ACCEPTABLE WORDS

Acceptable Words

Prayers for the Writer

Edited by

Gary D. Schmidt
Elizabeth Stickney

William B. Eerdmans Publishing Company

Grand Rapids, Michigan / Cambridge, U.K.

Published 2012 by
Wm. B. Eerdmans Publishing Co.
2140 Oak Industrial Drive N.E., Grand Rapids, Michigan 49505 /
P.O. Box 163, Cambridge CB3 9PU U.K.

Printed in the United States of America

18 17 16 15 14 13 12   7 6 5 4 3 2 1

Library of Congress Cataloging-in-Publication Data

Acceptable words : prayers for the writer /
edited by Gary D. Schmidt, Elizabeth Stickney.
p.   cm.
Includes bibliographical references and index.
ISBN 978-0-8028-6879-4 (pbk. : alk. paper)
1. Authors — Prayers and devotions.
I. Schmidt, Gary D.   II. Stickney, Elizabeth.
BV4596.A85A33 2012
242'.68 — dc23

2012027419

www.eerdmans.com

To Leonard and Sue Kuyvenhoven

and

Ruth and Greg Boven,

with prayers of thanks

Contents

The soul of Man must quicken to creation.
Out of the formless stone, when the artist united himself
with stone,
Spring always new forms of life, from the soul of man
that is joined to the soul of stone;
Out of the meaningless practical shapes of all that is living
or lifeless,
Joined with the artist's eye, new life, new form, new colour.
Out of the sea of sound the life of music,
Out of the slimy mud of words, out of the sleet and hail of
verbal imprecisions,
Approximate thoughts and feelings, words that have taken
the place of thoughts and feelings,
There spring the perfect order of speech, and the beauty
of incantation.

T. S. ELIOT

When we see any man doe any work well, that belongs to the
hand, to write, to carve, to play, to doe any mechanique office
well . . . doe we not rather raise our contemplation to the soule,
and her faculties, which enable that hand to do that work?

JOHN DONNE

You say grace before meals.
All right.
But I say grace before the play and the opera,
And grace before the concert and pantomime,
And grace before I open a book,
And grace before sketching, painting,
Swimming, fencing, boxing, watching, playing, dancing;
And grace before I dip the pen in the ink.

G. K. CHESTERTON

General Introduction

Let the words of my mouth,
and the meditations of my heart,
be acceptable in thy sight,
O LORD, my strength, and my redeemer.

PSALM 19.14 (KJV)

You have an idea for a screenplay, novel, blog, article, drama, biography, memoir, poem, short story, long epic. The premise sets up housekeeping in your mind among all your other thoughts and agendas. It occupies you, this germ of human expression. You arrange your affairs so that you have the time to write. It's a hard business, this arranging, so you spend hundreds of dollars to go to a retreat center, away from your normal routines. Now, back home, you clean your office again, and re-arrange the books that need re-arranging. Then you sit at your desk in your comfortable chair. Perhaps your son-in-law builds a fire in the woodstove to keep you warm. You sharpen your pencils, change the ribbon in the Royal typewriter, power up your laptop.

And you set out to write.

Except that the words do not flow as you had pictured them. After a couple of hours, you're looking at only a meager couple of paragraphs. After lunch you decide to take a walk with the border collies under the pale autumn sun. When you return to your desk, your morning's effort looks insubstantial and shabby. Or pretentious and pointless. Unpolished and amateur. All of the above. You start to throw it away — and then stop. It's all you have, after all. It's something. Best to save it.

You start again.

If you were a writer in ancient Greece or Rome you would know the exact nature of your problem: you neglected to call down the power of the Muse. Homer opens *The Odyssey* by requesting the Muse to sing to him the story of Odysseus, so that in turn he can relate it to his hearers. Virgil begins the *Aeneid* with this plea: "O Muse! The causes and the crimes relate; / What goddess was provok'd, and whence her hate." So.

This style of invocation lasted a long time: "Look in thy heart and write," chides Sir Philip Sidney's Renaissance Muse. John Milton, writing even later in Puritan England, adopts this convention in the opening lines of *Paradise Lost*.

> Of Man's first disobedience, and the fruit
> Of that forbidden tree whose mortal taste
> Brought death into the World, and all our woe,
> With loss of Eden, till one greater Man
> Restore us, and regain the blissful Seat,
> Sing, Heavenly Muse. . . .

The contemporary writer who, like Milton, writes out of a faith tradition, might ask about the identity of Milton's Heavenly Muse. Was he addressing the Holy Spirit in these lines — the One who came down at Pentecost with tongues of fire and new words? Should I, too, invoke the Spirit of God to give me my best ideas? To enable me to write stanzas that make my reader nod in agreement and wonder at my capacities and craft? To write novels and poems that reviewers praise? Sentences that make my own spirit glad?

The Hebrew and Christian scriptures do not spend much time reflecting about the source of our writerly diction, the strategies of narrative point of view, the subtleties of tonality. Writers of the Biblical texts are more interested in immediately getting to the action of the story, exhorting the people of God to live lives of faithful obedience, or correcting mistaken teachings and assumptions that had taken hold in the community of believers. And those writers are interested, above all, in recording the incomparable works of the One who created our earth and gave us life and the ability to express our thoughts. "The earth is the LORD's, and the fullness thereof," the Psalmist writes. "O LORD our Lord, how excellent is thy name in all the earth!" And this: "The heavens declare the glory of God, and the firmament sheweth his handiwork."

Today's writer of faith echoes those sentiments in all earnestness and vigor. That writer, too, sees evidences of God's glory in nature, and wants to find appropriate words to describe it. That writer, too, wants to understand the world and each person's place in it. That writer, too, wants to understand the dynamics of community, and the tension of individual belief. That writer, too, wants to understand what it means to be a writer and to exercise the gift faithfully.

The writer of faith recognizes the call to live up to an identity as God's image-bearer; the writer recognizes the call to use words in ways that bring honor to the One who gave language; the writer recognizes the call to use all capacity to appreciate and create beauty; and the writer recognizes the call to offer up our small voices in the universal anthem of praise.

"Let the words of my mouth, and the meditations of my heart, be acceptable in thy sight, O LORD, my strength, and my redeemer." "Acceptable." A small prayer, a humble one, tucked at the end of a long psalm that praises God for his glory, that uses all the trappings of royalty to describe that glory, then extols the goodness of God's judgment and law. May my words be worthy to describe you, Lord. May they please you. May they reflect your glory. May they make a difference. May they do what they were intended to do.

Not all the prayers in this collection are addressed to God as the Heavenly Muse. Not all are focused on discovering the source of a writer's inspiration, or calling down the Spirit of God to aid the writer in his or her literary efforts. But all of them reflect the writer's attempt to understand what it means to live out a calling in this world of beauty, grace, and order — and ugliness, hatred, and chaos. These are prayers seeking to understand what it is to make our words "acceptable." How to do such a thing?

This is the problem with which David Head wrestles as he imagines St. Thomas Aquinas, the greatest of the Schoolmen, speaking in heaven:

In my writing on earth I sought Thy praise and glory, and seemed to receive Thy approval. Once Thou didst say to me, "Thomas, thou hast written well of Me. What reward desirest Thou?" My reply then is my reply now: "None, save Thyself, Lord."

Now, with the infinite knowledge of Heaven to enjoy, I see the real value of my human writings. I thank Thee that they are not forgotten, but still bring wisdom to man and glory to Thee. I pray that in every generation there may be those to interpret the eternal Gospel to their contemporaries as I sought to do. Yet even before that final 7th March, everything I had written seemed worthless beside what I had seen. Now I see in a new way. Now I see enough to turn me again into a dumb ox, praising Thee in silent wonder and clumsy motions. Through all eternity I shall be asking, "What is God?"

The answer to how to live out the gift faithfully, Head suggests, is right focus.

So with this vocation, and with this call, and with this gift, and with this focus, why are we writers not always eager to begin? Why do we keep sharpening the pencils and rearranging the books?

Christina Rossetti considers the problem this way:

Suppose our duty of the moment is to write: Why do we not write? — Because we cannot summon up anything original, or striking, or picturesque, or eloquent, or brilliant.

But is the subject set before us? — It is.

Is it true? — It is.

Do we understand it? — Up to a certain point we do.

Is it worthy of meditation? — Yes, and prayerfully.

Is it worthy of exposition? — Yes, indeed.

Why then not begin? —

There are many reasons why we do not begin. We anticipate that our vision will not match our production. We do not think we have the skill to solve the narrative problems of this piece. We do not believe we know enough. We are unable to find the time. We're not sure that this is our vocation. We are tired. We are afraid. We are really afraid.

And so we pray.

For when the writing day comes to an end, when we shut down the word processing program, put the vinyl cover back on the Royal, set the pencils back in the pencil holder our children made the summer they were four, and when we look at the word count for the day and it's not even close to what we had hoped for, and when we re-read our stuff and realize that we didn't manage to say something that might be unique and important — when all of this is done, then what matters is that we worked hard and faithfully at the task that we were called to do: to bring acceptable words into the world, to bring acceptable words into God's world.

This is what writers, who, as Paul reminds the church at Ephesus, "are God's workmanship," are called to do.

Why then not begin?

We offer here prayers from across the centuries, from writers traditional and orthodox and from writers who would not see themselves so. Perhaps most importantly, these are petitions from writers who turned to prayerful expressions to address the joys and problems that writing poses.

These are the prayers of those writers who came before us, and the prayers of those writing today. These are the prayers of those who love words and who love God's world and who love the ways in which the words and the world may come together. These prayers are acts of devotion, are expressions of frustration, are pleas for hope and understanding. These prayers are a yearning for words — the right words, the acceptable words.

The Writer Encounters the World

The heavens declare the glory of God; and the firmament
*   sheweth his handiwork.*
Day unto day uttereth speech, and night unto night
*   sheweth knowledge.*
There is no speech nor language, where their voice
*   is not heard.*
Their line is gone out through all the earth, and their
*   words to the end of the world.*

PSALM 19.1-4

S uppose, wonders Ralph Waldo Emerson in his essay, "Nature," suppose the stars came out only one night every thousand years. Suppose the night was drawing nigh. Would we not all be filled with a fantastic eagerness to see this strange thing, of which we had heard only the most ancient of stories? Would we not anticipate it, and wait breathlessly? And when we had seen these miraculous stars, would we not wonder and marvel at the display? Would we not write poetry about the sight? Would we not tell the tale to future generations, that we were alive on this once-in-a-millennium night, when all the stars of heaven poured light down upon earth?

But, says Emerson, the stars come out every night. Every night the starry heavens, with all their wonders, unfold to us, as we walk across the village commons. This is the miracle of the universe.

Or, as the Belgic Confession asserts, we know God "by the creation, preservation, and government of the universe, since that universe is before our eyes like a beautiful book in which all creatures, great and small, are as letters to make us ponder the invisible things of God: his eternal power and his divinity."

Writers, as Flannery O'Connor has said, begin with what is physical and concrete. They begin with their perceptions of the extraordinary, mundane, knowable, confusing, healing, broken, moving, exasperating world that we find around us. Our characters, our themes, our images, our settings, our plots, our metaphors, our language, our tones — all the elements that the writer crafts into a text — come out of that world. What else could a writer do?

It is the writer's task to stay peculiarly attached to and aware of the physical created world — and to be aware of the awareness. The writer is aware of the miracle of a maple tree bark, even though she may be in a forest of maple trees. The writer is aware

THE WRITER ENCOUNTERS THE WORLD

of the cracks in this one sidewalk he walks on, even though he is walking in a city of sidewalks. The writer is aware of the smell of salty pretzels, the beat of the sun at the high altitudes, the lonely cry of a train whistle across cornfields, the slight twist in the dying man's nose, the hosta mostly deer-eaten, the gait of the border collie, the pulled-back hair of the high school volleyball player, the bleary-eyed determination of this one girl with a head cold, trudging to school among all the other students.

The writer knows that the stars come out every night, that they are all around us, and that they are stars.

The Victorian essayist John Ruskin wrote in his 1872 lecture, "The Relation of Wise Art to Wise Science," that he had one urgent thing he wanted to tell all artists; it was this: "You cannot learn to love art, unless you first love what art mirrors."

Art — writing — mirrors the world, the world that, the Psalmist says, day after day pours forth speech, and night after night displays knowledge; its words go to the ends of the earth. This is the world the writer knows. This is the world from which the writer draws all matter. This is the world for which the writer feels gratitude and love.

I will thank God for the pleasures given me through my senses, for the glory of the thunder, for the mystery of music, the singing of birds and the laughter of children. I will thank God for the pleasures of seeing, for the delights through colour, for the awe of the sunset, the beauty of flowers, the smile of friendship, and the look of love; for the changing beauty of the clouds, for the wild roses in the hedges, for the form and beauty of birds, for the leaves on the trees in spring and autumn, for the witness of the leafless trees through the winter, teaching us that death is sleep and not destruction, for the sweetness of flowers and the scent of hay. Truly, oh Lord, the earth is full of Thy riches! And yet, how much more I will thank and praise God for the strength of my body enabling me to work, for the refreshment of sleep, for my daily bread, for the days of painless health, for the gift of my mind and the gift of my conscience, for his loving guidance of my mind ever since it first began to think, and of my heart ever since it first began to love.

Edward King

A Prayer in Spring

Oh, give us pleasure in the flowers today;
And give us not to think so far away
As the uncertain harvest; keep us here
All simply in the springing of the year.

Oh, give us pleasure in the orchard white,
Like nothing else by day, like ghosts by night;
And make us happy in the happy bees,
The swarm dilating round the perfect trees.
And make us happy in the darting bird
That suddenly above the bees is heard,
The meteor that thrusts in with needle bill,
And off a blossom in mid air stands still.

Robert Frost

God's World

O world, I cannot hold thee close enough!
   Thy winds, thy wide grey skies!
   Thy mists, that roll and rise!
Thy woods, this autumn day, that ache and sag
And all but cry with colour! That gaunt crag
To crush! To lift the lean of that black bluff!
World, World, I cannot get thee close enough!

Long have I known a glory in it all,
   But never knew I this;
   Here such a passion is
As stretcheth me apart, — Lord, I do fear
Thou'st made the world too beautiful this year;
My soul is all but out of me, — let fall
No burning leaf; prithee, let no bird call.

Edna St. Vincent Millay

Almighty God, dwelling in the beauty of holiness, from
whom all skills of mind, hand and tongue do come; may
those who give their lives to the creation of beauty be sur-
prised by the joy of discovering your presence in your
world, and give others the hope of beholding your glory
unveiled in heaven, where you are alive and reign, Creator,
Redeemer and Sanctifier, one God for ever and ever.

Michael John Radford Counsell

The heavens declare thy glory, Lord;
In every star thy wisdom shines;
But when our eyes behold thy word,
We read thy name in fairer lines.

Sun, moon, and stars convey thy praise
Round the whole earth, and never stand;
So, when thy truth began its race,
It touched and glanced on every land.

Nor shall thy spreading Gospel rest
Till through the world thy truth has run;
Till Christ has all the nations blest
That see the light or feel the sun.

Great Sun of Righteousness, arise;
Bless the dark world with heavenly light;
Thy Gospel makes the simple wise,
Thy laws are pure, thy judgements right;

Thy noblest wonders ere we view,
In souls renewed and sins forgiven;
Lord, cleanse my sins, my soul renew,
And make thy word my guide to heaven.

Isaac Watts

Ice Storm

Unable to sleep, or pray, I stand
by the window looking out
at moonstruck trees a December storm
has bowed with ice.

Maple and mountain ash bend
under its glassy weight,

their cracked branches falling upon
the frozen snow.

The trees themselves, as in winters past,
will survive their burdening,
broken thrive. And am I less to You,
my God, than they?

Robert Hayden

We thank thee, Lord, for the glory of the late days and the
excellent face of thy sun. We thank thee for good news received. We thank thee for the pleasures we have enjoyed
and for those we have been able to confer. And now, when
the clouds gather and the rain impends over the forest and
our house, permit us not to be cast down; let us not lose
the savour of past mercies and past pleasures; but, like the
voice of a bird singing in the rain, let grateful memory
survive in the hour of darkness. If there be in front of us
any painful duty, strengthen us with the grace of courage;
if any act of mercy, teach us tenderness and patience.

Robert Louis Stevenson

Our Father, forgive us for thinking small thoughts of you
and for ignoring your immensity and greatness.
Lord Jesus, forgive us when we forget that you rule
the nations and our small lives.
Holy Spirit, we offend you in minimizing your power
and squandering your gifts.
We confess that our blindness to your glory, O triune God,
has resulted in shallow confession,
tepid conviction, and only mild repentance.
Have mercy upon us.
In Jesus' name. Amen

The Worship Sourcebook

A Grace

God, I know nothing, my sense is all nonsense,
And fear of You begins intelligence:
Does it end there? For sexual love, for food,
For books and birch trees I claim gratitude,
But when I grieve over the unripe dead
My grief festers, corrupted into dread,
And I know nothing. Give us our daily bread.

Donald Hall

O God, we thank you for this earth, our home; for the wide sky and the blessed sun, for the salt sea and the running water, for the everlasting hills and the never-resting winds, for trees and the common grass underfoot.

We thank you for our senses by which we hear the songs of birds, and see the splendor of the summer fields, and taste of the autumn fruits, and rejoice in the feel of the snow, and smell the breath of the spring.

Grant us a heart wide open to all this beauty; and save our souls from being so blind that we pass unseeing when even the common thornbush is aflame with your glory, O God our creator, who lives and reigns for ever and ever.

Walter Rauschenbusch

i thank You God for most this amazing
day: for the leaping greenly spirits of trees
and a blue true dream of sky; and for everything
which is natural which is infinite which is yes

(i who have died am alive again today,
and this is the sun's birthday; this is the birth
day of life and of love and wings: and of the gay
great happening illimitably earth)

how should tasting touching hearing seeing
breathing any — lifted from the no

of all nothing — human merely being
doubt unimaginable You?

(now the ears of my ears awake and
now the eyes of my eyes are opened)

e. e. cummings

Triune God
Creator of heaven and earth
  Who formed out of nothing all that is
Spirit who moved across the face of the deep
  And breathed life into inanimate clay
  Wisdom, the master artist,
  Who delights in all that is made

We thank you for the beauty of this world
  And for the gifts you give to those who create beauty,
    Who craft the mirrors that reflect your glory,
    Prisms that refract your light into a thousand
      dancing colors.

Beauty will not save the world.
But you — who are all beauty — have redeemed us
  At the cost of your own son.
For out of Zion, the perfection of beauty, God has shined.

Late have we loved you, beauty so old and so new
But this we desire,
  That we may dwell in the house of the Lord all the days
    of our lives

To behold the beauty of the Lord
And to seek his face.

Today and every day
    May the beauty of the Lord our God be upon us
    To establish the work of our hands
    And the offering of our hearts.

Through the power of the Holy Spirit
And in the name of Christ Jesus our Lord.

Susan Felch

A Prayer to God the Father on the Vigil of Pentecost

Today, Father, this blue sky lauds you. The delicate green
and orange flowers of the tulip poplar tree praise you. The
distant blue hills praise you, together with the sweet-
smelling air that is full of brilliant light. The bickering fly-
catchers praise you with the lowing cattle and the quails
that whistle over there. I too, Father, praise you, with all
these my brothers, and they give voice to my own heart
and to my own silence. We are all one silence, and a diver-
sity of voices.

You have made us together, you have made us one and
many, you have placed me here in the midst as witness, as
awareness, and as joy. Here I am. In me the world is present, and you are present. I am a link in the chain of light
and of presence. You have made me a kind of center, but a
center that is nowhere. And yet also I am "here. . . ."

To be here with the silence of Sonship in my heart is to be a center in which all things converge upon you. That is surely enough for the time being.

Therefore, Father, I beg you to keep me in this silence so that I may learn from it the word of your peace and the word of your mercy and the word of your gentleness to the world: and that through me perhaps your word of peace may make itself heard where it has not been possible for anyone to hear it for a long time.

To study truth here and learn here to suffer for truth.

The Light itself, and the contentment and the Spirit, these are enough.

Thomas Merton

O God of the blue, red, brown, black, and multicolored bird, of the singing, humming, and silent bird, of the noisy woodpecker and cooing dove, of perfect yellow sunflowers, fanciful laughing pansies, and pungent purple lavender, thank You for Your beautiful gifts of rich difference and variety.

O God, whose countless shades of green we cannot discern, who made no two leaves, grasses, animals, or humans alike, who made blue sky, white and gray clouds, soft reddish-brown and black earthen soils, infinite desert sands and impenetrable oceans deep, we thank You for the manifold and diverse universe You have made and shared with us.

Marian Wright Edelman

This earth is ours to love: lute, brush and pen,
They are but tongues to tell of life sincerely;
The thaumaturgic Day, the might of men,
O God of Scribes, grant us to grave them clearly!
Grant heart that homes in heart, then all is well.
Honey is honey-sweet; howe'er the hiving.
Each to his work, his wage at evening bell
    The strength of striving.

Robert Service

2

The Writer Studies the World

When I consider thy heavens, the work of thy fingers,
the moon and the stars, which thou has ordained;
What is man, that thou art mindful of him?
And the son of man, that thou visitest him?

PSALM 8.3-4

Writers often work at imitating the world — mimesis. In this, the writer's task is to create in poetry or prose a credible representation of the real world, so that the characters seem to be real folks, who live and move and have their being in real settings, who respond to their environments in real ways, and to history in real ways.

Mimesis is an imitation of life.

For of course, art is not life. Art is life reconstructed and represented through the observant and trained eye of the artist. For the writer to reconstruct and represent, she must not only observe the world around her, but study it in all of its multiple parts, and study those who have studied it. A writer, observes Samuel Johnson, "will turn over half a library to make one book." Just so. That's about what it takes.

To learn of the world can be a maddening step for the writer, and certainly can be a quagmire. There will always be another book to turn to before writing; there will always be another article to read, another fact to check. How many writers get so caught up in learning about the world of the book, that they never get to the book itself?

One of the characters in what may be the loveliest — and probably one of the more underestimated — of the Golden Era Hollywood Christmas films, *The Bishop's Wife,* is an aged professor, who has spent years and years researching his history of Rome. He has so choked himself with his research that he no longer has the ability to write his book; the whole enterprise has become dry as dust. It takes angelic influence — the angel played by Cary Grant — to suggest to the professor that his book is about story, and that the whole endeavor is most worthy when it is most story-like. And to his despair that he is old and past his possibilities, angel Cary reassures him, "You'll have time, Professor," and he hands him an ancient coin that sparks an outpouring of narrative.

Sometimes it takes angelic interposition.

The writer learns about the world in the service of his art. In doing this, the writer comes to recognize in ways impossible through observation only, the interrelatedness and complexity and associative quality of the created world. And this complexity must undergird her work, like a strong and sturdy cement foundation undergirds a building of steel and glass, and gives it shape, support, and being.

Turning over half the library so as to get the foundation right and true — that's a daunting task for the writer. But all authentic art exists only because of it.

O Lord our God! thou art teaching us through thy written word, that we may know how to understand thy created revelation. Grant, we beseech thee, that we may know the beginning of all knowledge of God, by the implanted spirit of God in us. We pray that thou wilt cleanse our souls from the darkness of nature; that thou wilt brood upon us, and bring from chaos out of the furnace of creation all ordered things.

Henry Ward Beecher

Thou who sendest forth the light, createst the morning, makest the sun to rise on the good and on the evil: enlighten the blindness of our minds with the knowledge of the truth: lift Thou up the light of Thy countenance upon us, that in Thy light we may see light, and, at the last, in the light of grace, (behold) the light of glory.

Lancelot Andrewes

Lord, my maker and protector, who has graciously sent me into this world, to work out my salvation, enable me to drive from me all such unquiet and perplexing thoughts as may mislead or hinder me in the practice of those duties which you have required. When I behold the works of your hands and consider the course of your providence, give me grace always to remember that your thoughts are not my thoughts, nor your ways my ways. And while it shall please you to continue me in this world where much is to be done and little to be known, teach me by your Holy Spirit to withdraw my mind from unprofitable and dangerous enquiries, from difficulties vainly curious and doubts impossible to be solved. Let me rejoice in the light which you have imparted, let me serve you with active zeal and humble confidence, and wait with patient expectation for the time in which the soul which you receive shall be satisfied with knowledge. Grant this, O Lord, for Jesus Christ's sake.

Samuel Johnson

O Thou who through the light of nature hast aroused in us a longing for the light of grace, so that we may be raised in the light of Thy majesty, to Thee I give thanks, Creator and Lord, that Thou allowest me to rejoice in Thy works. Praise the Lord ye heavenly harmonies, and ye who know the revealed harmonies. For from Him, through Him and in Him, all is, which is perceptible as well as spiritual; that which we know and that which we do not know, for there is still much to learn.

Johannes Kepler

Most Gracious and Holy Father,
give us wisdom to perceive you,
intelligence to understand you,
diligence to seek you,
patience to wait for you,
eyes to behold you,
a heart to meditate on you,
and a life to proclaim you,
through the power of the Holy Spirit
and the love of Jesus Christ, our Lord.

Frank Topping

I have work to do, I have a busy world around me; eye, ear, and thought will be all needed for that work, done in and amidst that busy world; now, ere I enter upon it, I would commit eye, ear, thought, and wish to thee. Do thou bless them and keep their work thine; that as, through thy natural laws, my heart beats and my blood flows without my thought for them, so my spiritual life may hold on its course through thy help, at those times when my mind cannot consciously turn to thee to commit each particular thought to thy service.

Thomas Arnold

Holy and undivided Trinity, unfailing Goodness, be present to my supplications, that as Thou hast made me partaker of Thy Sacraments, for no merits of mine own, but of Thy sole and undeserved Bounty, so even until that hour, when I am to depart hence, Thou wouldst make me to persevere in Faith, and Hope, and Charity; protect and defend me from all evil; grant unto me all that may profit me; free me from everlasting punishment, and bring me to unending joys; and henceforth make to cease that deadly temptation of the devil, which for my sins I fear may prevail against me. O God, Three-fold and One, accept now the prayers of Thy humble servant. Give me, O Lord, diligence to seek Thee; wisdom to find Thee; a soul to acknowledge Thee; eyes to see Thee; a conversation well-pleasing to Thee. . . . Purify my mind; sanctify my life; amend my habits; enlighten my heart with Heavenly Wisdom; let words of truth and mercy, kindness and concord, proceed out of my mouth. O Lord, make me to persevere unto the end, and give me that perfect end.

St. Anselm

A Hymn

O God of earth and altar,
Bow down and hear our cry,
Our earthly rulers falter,
   Our people drift and die;
The walls of gold entomb us,
   The swords of scorn divide,
Take not thy thunder from us,
   But take away our pride.

From all that terror teaches,
From lies of tongue and pen,
From all the easy speeches
   That comfort cruel men,
From sale and profanation
   Of honour and the sword,
From sleep and from damnation,
   Deliver us, good Lord.

Tie in a living tether
The prince and priest and thrall,
Bind all our lives together,
   Smite us and save us all;
In ire and exultation
   Aflame with faith, and free,
Lift up a living nation,
   A single sword to thee.

G. K. Chesterton

Almighty God, our heavenly Father, without whose help labour is useless, without whose light search is vain, invigorate my studies, and direct my inquiries, that I may, by due diligence and right discernment, establish myself and others in thy Holy Faith. Take not, O Lord, thy Holy Spirit from me; let not evil thought have dominion in my mind. Let me not linger in ignorance, but enlighten and support me, for the sake of Jesus Christ our Lord. Amen.

Samuel Johnson

To God the Father, God the Word, God the Spirit, we pour forth most humble and hearty supplications; that He, remembering the calamities of mankind and the pilgrimage of this our life, in which we wear out days few and evil, would please to open to us new refreshments out of the fountains of his goodness, for the alleviating of our miseries. This also we humbly and earnestly beg, that Human things may not prejudice such as are Divine; neither that from the unlocking of the gates of sense, and the kindling of a greater natural light, anything of incredulity or intellectual night may arise in our minds towards the Divine Mysteries. But rather that by our mind thoroughly cleansed and purged from fancy and vanities, and yet sub-

THE WRITER STUDIES THE WORLD

ject and perfectly given up to the Divine Oracles, there
may be given unto Faith the things that are Faith's.

Francis Bacon

A Writer's Prayer in Autumn

Creator God,

Thank you for that tree,
the small one, with low
branches holding tight
to its leaves, orange
fringed with yellow,
fiery tongues suspended
from brittle stems.

And around that tree,
the small one, circled thick
trunks with bare limbs,
a company of quiet maples,
empty and still
after layering
the grass gold.

Forgive me for only slowing
my hurried pace,
forgive me
I should have stopped,
taken off my shoes

and knelt.
But I rushed on
to important things,
things I have now forgotten.

Give me the eyes
to notice and let
my words catch
color and flame,
fall and float
brightly on a page,
so I may stand
empty handed,
pointing to you.

Otto Selles

My heart, speak now to God and say this: "I look for Your
face, O Lord; it is Your face I look for. O Lord my God,
teach my heart where to seek You and how to seek You,
and where to find You and how to find You. . . . Since I am
bent and bowed over, I can only look down; raise me and
straighten me, so that I may look up. . . . Teach me to look
for You, and show Yourself to me, for I cannot seek You
unless You teach me how to seek You, nor find You unless
You Yourself, reveal Yourself. I give thanks, O Lord, that
You have created Your image in me; because of Your image, I may remember, and think of, and love You. But Your
image in me is so worn away by sin, so hidden by sin's

THE WRITER STUDIES THE WORLD

smoke, that unless You renew and reform it, it cannot do what You created it to do. So I do not try for, Lord, Your high places; my understanding is not equal to that leap. But I do try to understand Your truth, the truth that my heart believes, and the truth that my heart loves. And therefore I say this: I do not seek to understand so that I may believe, but I believe so that I may understand.

St. Anselm

O Infinite Creator, who in the riches of Thy wisdom didst appoint three hierarchies of Angels and didst set them in wondrous order over the highest heavens, and who didst apportion the elements of the world most wisely: do Thou, who are in truth the fountain of light and wisdom, deign to shed upon the darkness of my understanding the rays of Thine infinite brightness, and remove far from me the twofold darkness in which I was born, namely, sin and ignorance. Do Thou, who givest speech to the tongues of little children, instruct my tongue and pour into my lips the grace of Thy benediction. Give me keenness of apprehension, capacity for remembering, method and ease in learning, insight in interpretation, and copious eloquence in speech. Instruct my beginning, direct my progress, and set Thy seal upon the finished work, Thou, who art true God and true Man, who livest and reignest, world without end.

Thomas Aquinas

Come, O my dear Lord, and teach me. . . . I need thee to teach me day by day, according to each day's opportunities and needs. . . . I need Thee to give me that true Divine instinct about revealed matters that, knowing one part, I may be able to anticipate or to approve of others. I need that understanding of the truths about Thyself which may prepare me for all Thy other truths — or at least may save me from conjecturing wrongly about them or commenting falsely upon them. . . . In all I need to be saved from an originality of thought, which is not true if it leads away from Thee. Give me the gift of discriminating between true and false in all discourse of mind. And, for that end, give me, O my Lord, that purity of conscience which alone can receive, which alone can improve Thy inspirations. My ears are dull, so that I cannot hear Thy voice. My eyes are dim, so that I cannot see Thy tokens. Thou alone canst quicken my hearing, and purge my sight, and cleanse and renew my heart. Teach me, like Mary, to sit at Thy feet, and to hear Thy word. Give me that true wisdom, which seeks Thy will by prayer and meditation, by direct intercourse with Thee, more than by reading and reasoning. Give me the discernment to know Thy voice from the voice of strangers, and to rest upon it and to seek it in the first place, as something external to myself; and answer me through my own mind, if I worship and rely on Thee and above and beyond it.

John Henry Newman

Dear Lord and Father of mankind,
Forgive our foolish ways!
Reclothe us in our rightful mind;
In purer lives Thy service find,
In deeper reverence, praise.

In simple trust like theirs who heard,
Beside the Syrian sea,
The gracious calling of the Lord,
Let us, like them, without a word
Rise up and follow Thee.

O Sabbath rest by Galilee!
O calm of hills above,
Where Jesus knelt to share with Thee
The silence of eternity,
Interpreted by love!

With that deep hush subduing all
Our words and works that drown
The tender whisper of Thy call,
As noiseless let Thy blessing fall
As fell Thy manna down.

Drop Thy still dews of quietness,
Till all our strivings cease:
Take from our souls the strain and stress;
And let our ordered lives confess
The beauty of Thy peace.

Breathe through the pulses of desire
Thy coolness and Thy balm;

Let sense be dumb, its heats expire:
Speak through the earthquake, wind, and fire,
O still small voice of calm!

John Greenleaf Whittier

Lord Jesus Merciful and Patient, grant us grace, I beseech
Thee, ever to teach in a teachable spirit; learning along
with those we teach, and learning from them whenever
Thou so pleasest. Word of God, speak to us, speak by us,
what Thou wilt. Wisdom of God, instruct us, instruct by us
if and whom Thou wilt. Eternal Truth, reveal Thyself to
us, reveal Thyself by us, in whatsoever measure Thou wilt.

Christina Rossetti

O unknown Love! We are inclined to think that your marvels are over, and that all we can do is to copy the ancient
Scriptures and quote your words from the past. We fail to
see that your inexhaustible action is the source of new
thoughts, new sufferings, new actions, new leaders, new
prophets, new apostles, new saints, who have no need to
copy each other's lives and writings, but live in perpetual
self-abandonment to your operations. We hear perpetually
of the "early centuries" and the "times of the saints." What

THE WRITER STUDIES THE WORLD

a way to talk! Are not all times and all events the successive results of your grace, pouring itself forth on all instants of time, filling them and sanctifying them? Your divine action will continue until the world ends to shed its glory on those souls who abandon themselves to your providence without reserve.

Jean Pierre de Caussade

Great are you, O Lord, and greatly to be praised. Great is your power; your wisdom is infinite. All people, as part of your creation, desire to praise you; all people, who carry the signs of mortality and sin, desire to praise you still. You provoke us toward that delight, for you have created us for yourself, and our hearts cannot be quieted until they find rest in you. . . . You will I seek, O Lord, calling upon you; you will I call, believing in you.

St. Augustine

O Lord, who by Thy holy Apostle hast taught us to do all things in the name of the Lord Jesus and Thy glory, give Thy blessing, we pray Thee, to this our daily work, that we may do it in faith, and heartily, as to the Lord and not unto men. All our powers of body and mind are Thine, and we would fain devote them to Thy service. Sanctify

them and the work in which they are engaged; let us not
be slothful, but fervent in spirit, and do Thou, O Lord, so
bless our efforts that they may bring forth in us the fruits
of true wisdom. Strengthen the faculties of our minds and
dispose us to exert them, but let us always remember to
exert them for Thy glory, and for the furtherance of Thy
kingdom, and save us from all pride, and vanity, and reli-
ance upon our own power or wisdom. Teach us to seek after truth, and enable us to gain it; but grant that we may
ever speak the truth in love: — that, while we know
earthly things, we may know Thee, and be known by
Thee, through and in Thy Son Christ. Give us this day Thy
Holy Spirit, that we may be Thine in body and spirit, in all
our work and all our refreshments, through Jesus Christ
Thy Son, Our Lord.

Thomas Arnold

My God, where is that ancient heat towards thee,
Wherewith whole shoals of martyrs once did burn,
Besides their other flames? Doth poetry
Wear Venus' livery? only serve her turn?
Why are not sonnets made of thee? and lays
Upon thine altar burnt? Cannot thy love
Heighten a spirit to sound out thy praise
As well as any she? Cannot thy Dove
Outstrip their Cupid easily in flight?
Or, since thy ways are deep, and still the fame,
Will not a verse run smooth that bears thy name!

Why doth that fire, which by thy power and might
Each breast does feel, no braver fuel choose
Than that, which one day, worms may chance refuse.

Sure Lord, there is enough in thee to dry
Oceans of ink; for, as the Deluge did
Cover the earth, so doth thy Majesty:
Each cloud distills thy praise, and doth forbid
Poets to turn it to another use.
Roses and lilies speak thee; and to make
A pair of cheeks of them, is thy abuse.
Why should I women's eyes for crystal take?
Such poor invention burns in their low mind
Whose fire is wild, and doth not upward go
To praise, and on thee, Lord, some ink bestow.
Open the bones, and you shall nothing find
In the best face but filth; when Lord, in thee
The beauty lies in the discovery.

George Herbert

Gracious Lord, grant that our work being done, and the
books crost in the time of our healths, we may be com-
forted when we come to dye, and to resign our souls into
the hands of a faithfull Creator and gracious redeemer. . . .
Lord, what particulars we pray for, we know not, we dare
not, we humbly tender a blank into the hands of almighty
God; write therein, Lord, what thou wilt, where thou wilt,

by whom thou wilt, only in thine own time work out
thine own honour and glory.

Thomas Fuller

O God, creation's secret force,
Thyself unmoved, all motion's source,
Who from the morn till evening ray,
Through all its changes guidest the day.

Come, Holy Ghost, with God the Son
And God the Father, ever one;
Shed forth Thy grace within our breast,
And dwell with us a ready guest.

By every power, by heart and tongue,
By act and deed, Thy praise be sung;
Inflame with perfect love each sense,
That others' souls may kindle thence.

O Father, that we ask be done
Through Jesus Christ, Thine only Son.
Who, with the Holy Ghost, and Thee
Still live and reign eternally.

St. Ambrose

Eternal God, grant that we may count it a day wasted when
we do not learn something new, and when we are not
a little further on the way to goodness and to Thee.
Help us to try to do our work better every day.
Help us to try to add something to our store of knowledge
every day.
Help us to try to know some one better every day.

Grant unto us each day to learn more of self-mastery and
self control.
Grant unto us each day better to rule our temper and our
tongue.
Grant unto us each day to leave our faults farther behind
and to grow more nearly into the likeness of our
Lord.
So grant that at the end of this day, and at the end of every
day, we may be nearer to Thee than when the day
began: through Jesus Christ our Lord.

William Barclay

God, who stretched the spangled heavens
Infinite in time and place,
Flung the suns in burning radiance
Through the silent fields of space,
We, Thy children, in Thy likeness,

Share inventive powers with Thee —
Great Creator, still creating,
Teach us what we yet may be.

We have conquered worlds undreamed of
Since the childhood of our race,
Known the ecstasy of winging
Through uncharted realms of space,
Probed the secrets of the atom,
Yielding unimagined power —
Facing us with life's destruction
Or our most triumphant hour.

As Thy new horizons beckon,
Father, give us strength to be
Children of creative purpose,
Serving man and honoring Thee.
'Til our dreams are rich with meaning —
Each endeavor Thy design —
Great Creator, lead us onward
'Til our work is one with Thine.

Catherine Cameron

Father in heaven! Show us a little patience; for we often intend in all sincerity to commune with Thee and yet we
speak in such a foolish fashion. Sometimes, when we judge
that what has come to us is good, we do not have enough
words to thank Thee; just as a mistaken child is thankful
for having gotten his own way. Sometimes things go so

badly that we call upon Thee; we even complain and cry
unto Thee; just as an unreasoning child fears what would
do him good. Oh, but if we are so childish how far from
being true children of Thine who are our true Father, ah,
as if an animal would pretend to have man as a father.
How childish we are and how little our proposals and our
language resemble the language which we ought to use
with Thee, we understand at least that it ought not to be
thus and that we ought to be otherwise. Have then a little
patience with us.

Søren Kierkegaard

God be in my head, and in my understanding;
God be in my eyes, and in my looking;
God be in my mouth, and in my speaking;
God be in my heart, and in my thinking;
God be at my end, and at my departing.

Sarum Primer (1538)

≈ 3 ≈

The Writer Begins

*Then the word of the LORD came unto me, saying,
Before I formed thee in the belly I knew thee; and
before thou cameth forth out of the womb I sanc-
tified thee, and I ordained thee a prophet unto the
nations. Then said I, Ah, Lord GOD! behold, I cannot speak: for I am a child. But the LORD said
unto me, Say not, I am a child: For thou shalt go
to all that I shall send thee, and whatsoever I
command thee, thou shalt speak. Be not afraid of
their faces: for I am with thee to deliver thee, saith
the LORD. Then the LORD put forth his hand, and
touched my mouth. And the LORD said unto me,
Behold, I have put my words in thy mouth.*

JEREMIAH 1.4-9

There is a story about Winston Churchill — who knows if it is true — that puts him in his garden, an easel and empty canvas in front of him, paralyzed because he is unable to brush that first stroke on his perfect, clean, undefiled white canvas. His neighbor, the story goes, finds him, and in exasperation, she takes the brush from his hand, dips it in bright red paint, and scrawls a curving line across the canvas.

And after this, Churchill can begin.

Most writers know the terror of the empty page — especially the first empty page of a new, long work — or what the writer hopes might become a new, long work. How does the writer get past the blankness?

First, the writer must say "Yes." "What would have happened to Mary (and to all the rest of us)," asks Madeleine L'Engle, "if she had said *No* to the angel? She was free to do so. But she said, *Yes.* She was obedient, and the artist, too, must be obedient to the command of the work, knowing that this involves long hours of research, of throwing out a month's work, or going back to the beginning, or, sometimes, scrapping the whole thing." Saying "Yes" does not mean a glib diving into a piece, though; usually it means an engaged commitment to the project — and to all its pain and joy and suffering. And sometimes saying "Yes" means a willingness to move away, to let go of the work and give it time to lie fallow, with the hope — the desperate hope — that something may indeed grow from that fallow, yet fertile, ground. But either way, we begin with affirmation.

Or perhaps we may put it this way: Our entry into the work is, first, through humility: "I will meekly bring my present," offers Christopher Smart. Or perhaps it is through a sense of calling and vocation: "Doing all things for thy glory here," whispers Jeremy Taylor. Or perhaps it is through a sense that the writerly skills are gifts of God, and so holy and not to be misused: "Instruct our speech, O God," begs Aquinas. Or perhaps it is through sheer hope: "May you guide the beginning of our work," prays Aquinas again. All of these are ways of saying "Yes."

Beginning a work is, as any writer knows, a plunge into experiment, first ideas, drafts, possibilities. In this, beginning a new page is like faith, which begins with hope, and grows to . . . greater hope, perhaps even a kind of certainty.

Writing workshops are often marked with Q and A's that include this question: "How do I begin?" The answer is really simple. You begin. Will you falter? Yes. Will you misstep? Yes. Will you have to turn around and start again? Yes and yes.

Will all of this be frustrating? Yes.

But how powerfully the process of writing mirrors the spiritual life, which calls for such elements as a faith that dares to begin, a strong perseverance despite our faltering missteps, and a repentance that turns back and starts again.

Writers know the principle.

A Poet's Prayer

God, you who by your word renew every good thing, take my dead tongue and make it vital. Enliven my speech this day that I might maneuver nouns, verbs, and particles into patterns not yet seen — poems that surprise the mind and quicken the heart, verses that are congruent with whatever is true. Inspire my imagination as I play with lines and reckon with sorrow that I might feel your pleasure. And when my words at last are revised, lead them invisibly to their audience. Amen.

L. S. Klatt

Lord, to the end that my heart may think, that my pen may write, and that my mouth may set forth Thy praise, pour forth into my heart and pen and mouth Thy grace.

Bernard of Cluny

Neither purse nor scrip I carry,
  But the books of life and pray'r;
Nor a staff my foe to parry,
  'Tis the cross of Christ I bear.

From a heart serene and pleasant
  'Midst unnumber'd ills I feel,
I will meekly bring my present,
  And with sacred verses kneel.

Muse, through Christ the Word, inventive
  Of the praise so greatly due;
Heav'nly gratitude retentive
  Of the bounties ever new,

Fill my heart with genuine treasures,
  Pour them out before his feet,
High conceptions, mystic measures,
  Springing strong and flowing sweet.

Grace, thou source of each perfection,
  Favour from the height thy ray;
Thou the star of all direction,
  Child of endless truth and day.

Thou that bidst my cares be calmer,
  Lectur'd what to seek and shun,
Come, and guide a western palmer
  To the Virgin and her Son.

Lo! I travel in the spirit,
  On my knees my course I steer

To the house of might and merit
  With humility and fear.

Poor at least as John or Peter
  I my vows alone prefer;
But the strains of love are sweeter
  Than the frankincense and myrrh.

Christopher Smart

O eternal God, who hast made all things for man, and man
for thy glory, Sanctify my body and soul, my thoughts and
my intentions, my words and actions, That whatsoever I
shall think, or speak, or do, may be by me designed to the
glorification of thy name; And by thy blessing it may be
effective and successful in the work of God, according as it
can be capable. Lord, turn my necessities into virtue; the
works of nature into the works of grace, by making them
orderly, regular, temperate, subordinate, and profitable to
ends beyond their own proper efficacy; and let no pride or
self-seeking, no covetousness or revenge, no impure mix-
ture or unhandsome purposes, no little ends or low imagi-
nations, pollute my spirit, and unhallow any of my words
and actions: but let my body be a servant to my spirit, and
both body and spirit servants of Jesus, that, doing all
things for thy glory here, I may be partaker of thy glory
hereafter, through Jesus Christ our Lord.

Jeremy Taylor

Heavenly Father, I am grateful for the opportunity to be a writer and to share my words and ideas with others. I thank Thee for allowing me the opportunity to be, in small part, as Thou art: a creator. I'm grateful too for the blessings that flow from editors, publishers, and of course, from readers. As I begin this new project, I am filled with self-doubt, second thoughts, and outright fear. Please give me the strength to take this leap of faith and the courage to face the blank page. My fear of the unknown leaves me crippled, blocked, wordless. Grant me the faith — no, the sure knowledge — that if I will put my trust in Thee and write even one sentence, a second will surely follow.

Chris Crowe

Thank you, God, for my little flask of oil —
A nub of pencil, the back of an envelope, a moment
    of quiet —
That I use to describe the room, start the conversation,
    tighten the action.
A few inches of text, new or better, are enough for today,
And more than enough to give me hope for oil in my flask
    tomorrow.

Elizabeth Vander Lei

The Writer's Prayer

Open my mind, Lord. Grant me the talent to write with
clarity and style, so my words go down rich and
smooth, like fine wine, and leave my reader thirsty
for more.

Open my heart, Lord. Grant me the sensitivity to
understand my characters — their hopes, their wants,
their dreams — and help me to confer that empathy
to my reader.

Open my soul, Lord, so I may be a channel to wisdom and
creativity from beyond my Self. Stoke my
imagination with vivid imagery and vibrant
perception.

But most of all, Lord, help me to know the Truth, so my
fiction is more honest than actuality and reaches the
depths of my reader's soul.

Wrap these gifts with opportunity, perseverance, and the
strength to resist those who insist it can't be done.

Sandy Tritt

Flickering Mind

Lord, not you,
it is I who am absent.

At first
belief was a joy I kept in secret,
stealing alone
into sacred places:
a quick glance, and away — and back,
circling.
I have long since uttered your name
but now
I elude your presence.
I stop
to think about you, and my mind
at once
like a minnow darts away,
darts
into the shadows, into gleams that fret
unceasing over
the river's purling and passing.
Not for one second
will my self hold still, but wanders
anywhere,
everywhere it can turn. Not you,
it is I am absent.
You are the stream, the fish, the light,
the pulsing shadow,
you the unchanging presence, in whom all
moves and changes.
How can I focus my flickering, perceive
at the fountain's heart
the sapphire I know is there?

Denise Levertov

Almighty God, in Whose hands are all the powers of man; Who givest understanding, and takest it away; Who, as it seemeth good unto Thee, enlightenest the thoughts of the simple, and darkenest the meditations of the wise, be present with me in my studies and enquiries.

Grant, O Lord, that I may not lavish away the life which Thou hast given me on useless trifles, nor waste it in vain searches after things which Thou hast hidden from me.

Enable me, by Thy Holy Spirit, so to shun sloth and negligence, that every day I may discharge part of the task which Thou hast allotted me; and so further with Thy help that labour which, without Thy help, must be ineffectual, that I may obtain, in all my undertakings, such success as will most promote Thy glory, and the salvation of my own soul, for the sake of Jesus Christ.

Samuel Johnson

May Your Spirit guide my mind,
Which is so often dull and empty.
Let my thoughts be always on You,
And let me see You in all things.

May Your Spirit quicken my soul,
Which is so often listless and lethargic.
Let my soul be awake to Your presence,
And let me know You in all things.

May Your Spirit melt my heart,
Which is so often cold and indifferent.
Let my heart be warmed by Your love,
And let me feel You in all things.

Johann Freylinghausen

Enable me, O God, to collect and compose my thoughts before an immediate approach to you in prayer. May I be
careful to have my mind in order when I take upon myself
the honour to speak to the Sovereign Lord of the universe,
remembering that upon the temper of my soul depends, in
very great measure, my success. You are infinitely too
great to be trifled with, too wise to be imposed on by a
mock devotion, and abhor a sacrifice without a heart. Help
me to entertain an habitual sense of your perfections, as an
admirable help against cold and formal performances.

Susanna Wesley

Almighty God, bestow upon us the meaning of words, the
light of understanding, the nobility of diction, and the
faith of the true nature. And grant that what we believe we
may also speak.

Hilary of Poitiers

Be on our lips, that we may speak no evil word.
Be in our eyes, that they may never linger on any
    forbidden thing.
Be on our hands, that we may do our own work with
    diligence, and serve the needs of others with
    eagerness.
Be in our minds, that no soiled or bitter thought may gain
    an entry to them.
Be in our hearts, that they may be warm with love for
    Thee, and for our fellow-men.

William Barclay

O Lord, guide my thoughts and my words. It is not that I
lack subjects for meditations. On the contrary, I am
crushed with the weight of them. . . . Now I am over-
whelmed by your blessings. O beloved Bridegroom there is
nothing that you have not done for me. Now tell me what
you want of me, how you expect me to serve you. Create in
my thoughts, words and actions that which will give true
glory to you.

Charles de Foucauld

I want to record you, observe you, describe —
not with cinnabar red and gold, just in ink of the apple
      tree's rind.
Even with beads I cannot tie you to the page,
and the most tottering image my senses contrive,
you blindly outdo by just being alive.

Rainer Maria Rilke

On all who are working with their hands: on all who are
studying and increasing knowledge: on all who are travel-
ling and trafficking, pour out, we pray Thee, Thy blessing. . . . And since it is only after labour that rest is sweet,
do Thou enable us to prepare for entering Thy rest by a
life of zeal and diligence. Whatever our hand findeth to do,
may we do it with our might. May we be earnest in purpose, fervent in spirit, serving Thee. Save each one of us
from listlessness and indolence. May we remember that
the time is short, and that the night cometh, when no man
can work. And thus, Lord, in faith and obedience, may we
wait for Thy salvation, and the final manifestation of Thy
children.

Henry Alford

Just give me a little more time!
I want to love the things
as no one has thought to love them,
until they're real and ripe and worthy of you.

I want only seven days, seven
on which no one has ever written himself —
seven pages of solitude.

There will be a book that includes these pages,
and she who takes it in her hands
will sit staring at it a long time.

until she feels that she is being held
and you are writing.

Rainer Maria Rilke

A Last Prayer

Father, I scarcely dare to pray,
   So clear I see, now it is done,
That I have wasted half my day,
   And left my work but just begun;

So clear I see that things I thought
   Were right or harmless were a sin;
So clear I see that I have sought,
   Unconscious, selfish aims to win;

So clear I see that I have hurt
  The souls I might have helped to save;
That I have slothful been, inert,
  Deaf to the calls thy leaders gave.

In outskirts of thy kingdoms vast,
  Father, the humblest spot give me;
Set me the lowliest task thou hast;
  Let me repentant work for thee!

Helen Hunt Jackson

On Prayer

Lord, I am slow
to speak
with You.
Not that You are
coins
to be cashed
in time
of need; not that
you are words
to cry or to sing.
It is just that it is a slow thing to speak
with anybody.

Colin Duriez

Hymn 15: Taste

1

O guide my judgement and my taste,
    Sweet SPIRIT, author of the book
Of wonders, told in language chaste
    And plainness, not to be mistook.

2

O let me muse, and yet at sight
    The page admire, the page believe;
"Let there be light, and there was light,
    Let there be Paradise and Eve!"

3

Who his soul's rapture can refrain?
    At Joseph's ever-pleasing tale
Of marvels, the prodigious train,
    To Sinai's hill from Goshen's vale.

4

The Psalmist and proverbial Seer,
    And all the prophets sons of song,
Make all things precious, all things dear,
    And bear the brilliant word along.

5

O take the book from off the shelf,
    And con it meekly on thy knees;
Best panegyric on itself,
    And self-avouch'd to teach and please.

6

Respect, adore it heart and mind.
How greatly sweet, how sweetly grand,
Who reads the most, is most refin'd,
And polish'd by the Master's hand.

Christopher Smart

Master

Your face is always just beyond
like a light in snow.
I cannot compare you, your hands,
your face to anything.

No symbol holds.
Yet you are no moth in frailty.
Your presence is flame and power.
And you are more solid than earth,
your hands more serviceable,
more human than mine.

Infinite gentleness, infinite power,
I love you like a fainting lover,
but my love poems are never enough.
For you are the poet, the lover,
and the poem.

Write Thou me.

Susan McCaslin

4

The Writer's Vision Expands

*Whoso offereth praise glorifieth me: and to him
that ordereth his conversation aright will I show
the salvation of God.*

PSALM 50.23

As college students, we would not infrequently take the train into Boston and head to the Isabella Stewart Gardner Museum — in the good old days, it was free on Sundays, and so a natural draw for poor students. There, we would go past the gardens, climb the broad marble stairs, head into a dark-tiled room, and stand before Rembrandt's "Christ on the Sea of Galilee," a masterpiece of epic proportion. On those Sundays, while the sun crossed the interior gardens below and behind us, we would stand there for a very long time.

It is an astonishing painting. The ship is slung out over towering and fraught waves, and the disciples are, well, going crazy — as are the distraught sailors. One is throwing up over the side; he looks like he wants to toss himself in and end it all. Deep in the hold, so deep that he is hardly visible in many prints of the painting, a red demon grins. But outside, in a whirl of bright light, Christ is utterly, utterly calm, perhaps just waking up. The master of waves and winds is unimpressed with a demon's skullduggery. He will deal with everything in a moment, he seems to say. Calm down. Relax. All shall be well, and all shall be well, and all manner of things shall be well.

The painting is gone now, stolen in one of America's most spectacular art thefts. Who knows if it hasn't been destroyed? But we still travel to that museum once a year — now with college students who are going, as we once did, for the first time. They climb the broad stairs with us, go into the dark-tiled room, and see us stand before the empty frame, which still hangs on the wall — a sign of hope. It gives the students one more reason to be quite sure that we are odd, standing there, in the middle of this room, looking at an empty frame. But they cannot know that when we stand there, we are seeing the painting as if it were on the wall; we are seeing every character, every glint of whirling light, the sinking ship, the wild ropes, the demon, the guy throwing up, and, most of all, the calm Christ. Hang on. It's all right. I'm here. The storm means nothing. I'm here.

Art drags us in through engagement — we are delighted, appalled, transfixed, amazed, puzzled, made giddily happy, saddened, moved. And art, after beginning with this inescapable capture, enlarges us. We are given greater understanding, we are given greater questions, we are given greater capacities. Art gives us, as Cornelius Plantinga has observed, more to be a human being with, and more to be a Christian with.

I do not know how much theology we learned on Sunday afternoons with Rembrandt. I think, a lot. I know it has given us more to be human beings with, and this, no theft can steal.

But here's something else to ponder: One of the mysteries of writing is that even as the writer seeks to pose questions and enlarge the reader, she herself is given questions, he himself is enlarged. The writer, seeking to illuminate, is illuminated.

If this is not grace, then no man ever wrote.

Lord, give us weak eyes
for things of little worth
and eyes clear-sighted
in all of your truth.

Søren Kierkegaard

With Thy Spirit with me, my words come without
    stammering. . . .
I would speak boldly, as I ought to speak.
I would learn the language of love.
I would praise Thee with the voice of mirth and
    thanksgiving.
I would pray with unsealed lips.
  Once I was dumb. Now, in Thy Presence, I speak plainly.

David Head

Kneeling

Moments of great calm,
Kneeling before an altar
Of wood in a stone church
In summer, waiting for the God
To speak; the air a staircase
For silence; the sun's light
Ringing me, as though I acted
A great rôle. And the audiences
Still; all that close throng
Of spirits waiting, as I,
For the message.
   Prompt me, God;
But not yet. When I speak,
Though it be you who speak
Through me, something is lost.
The meaning is in the waiting.

R. S. Thomas

What in me is dark, illumine,
What is low raise and support,
That to the height of this great argument
I may assert eternal Providence,
And justify the ways of God to men.

John Milton

Benediction

Let there be light in all the nightmare places,
in the millrace of license, in the stifled room;
let there be joy in starved and leaden faces,
in charred or sodden furrows, where no tears bloom.

Where stumbling feet, where fumbling hands are groping
against the scope of silence, in dumb primordial caves,
let chords of morning stars bring prismed hoping
and sing far up the slope, where mind blinds out and
     raves.

Say for me, God, their blessing I am seeking;
Lord, decree for them the sun, and Jesus speak aright
my scattered syllables — for past my yearning, past
     my speaking,
I have been stammering, let there be light.

William R. Mitchell

O most Holy, Almighty, Eternal, Divine Spirit, Who art of
     one Authority and Dominion with the Father and the
     Son; set up Thy throne in our hearts, indwell us,
     gather us into Thine obedience, reign over us.
Thou Who art Lord and Giver of Life, grant us life, a long
     life, even for ever and ever.

Thou Who art a Loving Spirit, ever willing to give Thyself
    to whoso will receive Thee, give Thyself to us, give
    Thyself to us more and more, and never withdraw
    Thyself from us.
Thou Who art Purity, purify us: Thou Who art Light,
    enlighten us: Thou Who art Fullness and
    Refreshment, make us Thine, keep us Thine, fill us,
    refresh us.
Thou Who lovest us, grant us grace to love Thee.
O Lord God Almighty, Most Holy Trinity, Jesus Christ is
    our sole plea for any gift, for any grace.

Christina Rossetti

Blessed you are, Lord God, King of the universe.
Blessed you are, ruler of all being,
God from the beginning and God in the end.
You are Lord of creation,
sending your Spirit to brood upon the deep
and giving to Adam the breath of life.

We bless you for the human spirit,
for the intelligence you have granted to us and to all
    humankind,
for the energy of our bodies, the strength of our arms,
for the determination of our wills, the power of our
    imagination.

We bless you that even in our fallen state we have a thirst
    for you.
We cry out for you.
Our spirits crave the anointing of your Spirit.

Blessed you are, Lord God of Israel,
calling the patriarchs and speaking through the prophets,
enlightening their visions, kindling their hope, teaching
    them wisdom.

Hughes Oliphant Old

Help the Blind

Heal me, O Jesus,
as you healed the blind:
Bethsaida's blind man,
Jericho's Bartimaeus.

Help me see gradually
if you desire
or in an instant of insight
if you choose.

But miracle my seeing
so I may
divine your grace
and join you in your journey.

Thomas John Carlisle

Father God, you are the Author of stories great and small.
Forgive me for sometimes thinking that inspiration comes
from only the great stories, the powerful narratives, the lyric
instances of profound beauty breaking forth on our senses.
Make me attentive, Lord, to all that may inspire in the quo-
tidian realities that surround me each day. Help me to listen
to the ordinary things people tell me. Make me attend to
how they speak and to the yearnings of their hearts that
emerge in such daily conversation. If I need fresh language
and new metaphors, let them emerge from the ordinary as
well as from the extraordinary so that the words I write may,
must so, speak strength and grace into the commonplaces of
people's lives. Your Son taught us that those who would be
truly great must humble themselves and be the servant of
all. In my writing, Lord God, give me a servant's heart so that
I may listen for also that beauty that emerges from even the
smallest voices of my everyday.

Scott Hoezee

Stay with me, and then I shall begin to shine as thou
shinest: so to shine as to be a light to others. The light, O
Jesus, will be all from Thee. None of it will be mine. No
merit to me. It will be Thou who shinest through me upon
others. O let me thus praise Thee, in the way which Thou
dost love best, by shining on all those around me. Give

THE WRITER'S VISION EXPANDS

light to them as well as to me; light them with me, through me. Teach me to show forth Thy praise, Thy truth, Thy will. Make me preach Thee without preaching — not by words, but by my example and by the catching force, the sympathetic influence, of what I do — by my visible resemblance to Thy saints, and the evident fullness of the love which my heart bears to Thee.

John Henry Newman

Let Thy Spirit be in our minds, to guide our thoughts
    towards the truth.
Let Thy Spirit be in our hearts, to cleanse them from every
    evil and unclean desire.
Let Thy Spirit be upon our lips, to preserve us from all
    wrong speaking, and to help us by our words to
    commend Thee unto others.
Let Thy Spirit be upon our eyes, that they may find no
    delight in looking on forbidden things, but that they
    may be fixed on Jesus.
Let Thy Spirit be upon our hands that they may be faithful
    in work and eager in service.

William Barclay

O Lord God, in whom we live and move and have our being, open our eyes that we may behold thy fatherly presence ever about us. Draw our hearts to thee with the power
of love. Teach us in nothing to be anxious; and when we
have done what thou hast given us to do, help us, O God
our Saviour, to leave the issue to thy wisdom. Take from us
all doubt and distrust. Lift our thoughts up to thee, and
make us know that all things are possible to us, in and
through thy Son our redeemer, Jesus Christ our Lord.

William Bright

Without Offerings

I am poor. I don't bring you
Any more offerings.
I come near you, empty-handed.
The phrases with their explained-away heads
I threw out long ago.
I know how you always rejoiced
In symbols.

As to sad synagogues,
To doorsteps of belief — How hard to come back
To old words.

I know well their places.
I hear their humming.
At times I get close, I look longingly
Through the windowpanes.

But you, still resting in the shadows of biblical trees,
Oh sing me chilly consolation
Of all that you remember, all that you know.

Jacob Glatshteyn

Huswifery

Make me, O Lord, Thy spinning wheel complete.
    Thy Holy Word my distaff make for me.
Make mine affections Thy swift flyers neat
    And make my soul Thy holy spool to be.
    My conversation make to be Thy reel
    And reel the yarn thereon spun of Thy wheel.

Make me Thy loom then; knit therein this twine;
    And make Thy Holy Spirit, Lord, wind quills;
Then weave the web Thyself. The yarn is fine.
    Thine ordinances make my fulling mills.
    Then dye the same in heavenly colors choice,
    All pinked with varnished flowers of Paradise.

Then clothe therewith mine understanding, will,
    Affections, judgment, conscience, memory,
My words and actions, that their shine may fill

My ways with glory and Thee glorify.
Then mine apparel shall display before ye
That I am clothed in holy robes for glory.

Edward Taylor

Lord Jesus,
write your truth in my mind, your joy in my heart, and
     your love in my life,
that filled with truth, possessed by joy, and living in love,
your integrity, your humour, and your compassion
might be born again in me.

Frank Topping

Vespers

Even as you appeared to Moses, because
I need you, you appear to me, not
often, however. I live essentially
in darkness. You are perhaps training me to be
responsive to the slightest brightening. Or, like the poets,
are you stimulated by despair, does grief
move you to reveal your nature? This afternoon,
in the physical world to which you commonly

contribute your silence, I climbed the small hill above the
    wild blueberries, metaphysically
descending, as on all my walks: did I go deep enough
for you to pity me, as you have sometimes pitied
others who suffer, favoring those
with theological gifts? As you anticipated,
I did not look up. So you came down to me:
at my feet, not the wax
leaves of the wild blueberry but your fiery self, a whole
pasture of fire, and beyond, the red sun neither falling nor
    rising —
I was not a child; I could take advantage of illusions.

Louise Glück

Almighty God, who hast sent the spirit of truth unto us to
guide us into all truth, so rule our lives by thy power, that
we may be truthful in word, deed and thought. O keep us,
most merciful Saviour, with thy gracious protection, that
no fear or hope may ever make us false in act or speech.
Cast out from us whatsoever loveth or maketh a lie, and
bring us all to the perfect freedom of thy truth; through
Jesus Christ our Lord. Amen.

William Bright

Forgive these wild and wandering cries,
Confusions of a wasted youth;
Forgive them where they fail in truth,
And in thy wisdom make me wise.

Alfred, Lord Tennyson

O Light Supreme, that dost so far uplift thee
    From the conceits of mortals, to my mind
    Of what thou didst appear re-lend a little,

And make my tongue of so great puissance,
    That but a single sparkle of thy glory
    It may bequeath unto the future people;

For by returning to my memory somewhat,
    And by a little sounding in these verses,
    More of thy victory shall be conceived! . . .

O how all speech is feeble and falls short
    Of my conceit, and this to what I saw
    Is such, 'tis not enough to call it little!

O light Eterne, sole in thyself that dwellest,
    Sole knowest thyself, and, known unto thyself
    And knowing, lovest and smilest on thyself!

Dante Alighieri

A Writer's Prayer after Psalm 144

> God of might and God of glory,
> Help me when I write for war.
> Let me see the way before me,
> Make me see what I am for.

Gracious God,

You know my heart and you know my vexations,
and you know better than I do what I am after.
Purify the source.

Give me clearer vision, so that I may see myself more
    clearly,
so that I may understand my desires more fully,
explore my virtues more carefully,
and know what battles must be fought.

And then guide my heart, Lord,
so that I fight real enemies and fight them the right way.
Purify the source.

Take away the ache, the hurt, the sullen wrath; take away
    the rage
that makes it impossible for me to see and hear and know
    things accurately.
Take away my willfulness, which distorts others and makes
    them worthy of destruction.

Train my hands for war, but let it be your war.
Destroy those who are full of deceit,

but have mercy on me when I fall short of the truth,
for I am small and broken and do not often know my true
    state.

We pray for sons and daughters full of grace,
for good harvests and for bounty,
for the city in which there is no cry of distress in the
    streets.

Bring all those blessings home to me:
Make me gracious, bountiful, peaceful, just.

Purify the source.

                                        James Vanden Bosch

No coward soul is mine,
No trembler in the world's storm-troubled sphere:
I see Heaven's glories shine,
And faith shines equal, arming me from fear.

O God within my breast,
Almighty, ever-present Deity!
Life — that in me has rest,
As I — undying Life — have Power in Thee!

Vain are the thousand creeds
That move men's hearts: unutterably vain;
Worthless as withered weeds,
Or idlest froth amid the boundless main,

To waken doubt in one
Holding so fast by thine infinity;

So surely anchored on
The steadfast rock of immortality.

With wide-embracing love
Thy spirit animates eternal years,
Pervades and broods above,
Changes, sustains, dissolves, creates, and rears.

Though earth and man were gone,
And suns and universes ceased to be,
And Thou wert left alone,
Every existence would exist in Thee.

There is not room for Death,
Nor atom that his might could render void:
Thou — Thou art Being and Breath,
And what Thou art may never be destroyed.

Emily Brontë

5

The Writer Attends to the Word

*Let my cry come near before thee, O LORD: give
me understanding according to thy word. Let my
supplication come before thee: deliver me according to thy word. My lips shall utter praise, when
thou hast taught me thy statutes. My tongue shall
speak of thy word: for all thy commandments are
righteousness.*

PSALM 119.169-172

B ernard Malamud once explained the process of the craft of writing: "You write by sitting down and writing." The writer Jane Yolen is more earthy. She has often said that the writer's most important rule is BOC — Butt on Chair. She may be right. Writing is a gift; writing is a skill; writing is a joy; writing is a sorrow. And writing is a discipline. It may be that there are some writers who are able to write in a white heat and produce reams with little effort, but one should not judge the profession through the aberrant. For most all of us, writing is a discipline that takes care and attention, with regular — we hope — sessions and regular — we hope — goals and regular — we hope — successes. For the writer, the pleasure of the rising pile of pages is the reward of discipline. (One more reason, as if we needed another, to abandon the electric chill of the word processor during composition.)

Of course, there are not always successes, and sometimes, often usually, the pile has to be pruned. BOC does not always mean finished pages at the end of the day. It may mean more cutting, more starting over.

But that, too, is attending to the word.

Occasionally it is a healthy thing for writers to look at the manuscripts of other writers; it is a practice that gives us hope. That repeated line at the end of "Stopping by Woods on a Snowy Evening" — that line that seems so inevitable now? That line wasn't repeated at first. It stood by itself, a little lonely and with a lot less punch. And Marley at the beginning of A Christmas Carol? He was almost "Old Marley," conjuring up images of a jovial, fun-loving, beloved bachelor rather than the chain-encrusted dead sinner.

We attend to the word.

We have held in our hands the light fascicles of Emily Dickinson's poems, the manuscript of Little Women, the revised journal pages Emerson used for his lectures, the autographs of John Greenleaf Whittier scissored from letters for a souvenir, Thoreau's handwritten poem, for sale in an upscale Boston bookstore, ready to go to the highest bidder — which probably will not be a library. All of these show the awful fragility of the writer's drafts. So much could so easily be lost. But for all writers, that page we work on, that page from a cheap tablet, from that black and white notebook, from that leather-bound journal — that page seems so incalculably valuable, and we cherish it and place it on our desk carefully because it contains the form and matter of our message to the world — even if it is a world that has never written back to us.

The writer attends to the word, and in so doing, brings out of the mess of ideas and the chaos of language and the upset of form, clarity and order and point. We write, to attend to the word. We attend to the word, to write.

For attending to the word means attending to the incarnation of the idea, the embodiment of the sentiment, the manifestation of the concept, the enfleshing of the meaning. It is to literally make physical the abstract. It is to bring into the world what was not in this form brought into the world before.

For the writer of faith, there is something awfully familiar about all of this — and mysterious, a mystery that Margaret Gibson expresses in "Poetry is the Spirit of the Dead, Watching."

What is prayer
if not a marriage
of passion and the opposing need
for quiet loneliness? What is
a poem, if not the death-cry
of each moment's hard-won
and abandoned self?

Creator and Redeemer God, your Word shows us that once those known as the disciples were prone to stammer and say all the wrong things. They asked your Son all the wrong questions. They rebuked those who brought children near. They scolded those who did great works in Jesus' name in case those wonder-workers were not part of the disciples' private club. But then your Spirit came in a Pentecostal out-pouring that somehow led to an eloquence, a boldness, an accuracy of expression the disciples could not have seen coming. Give me that Spirit, Lord my God! Untie my tongue, loosen my pen, set free my hands on the keyboard. Where before I have been foggy, let your Spirit's warm breath blow away the vapors and give me clarity. Where before I asked the wrong questions, give me the Spirit's epiphany to penetrate to right queries. Let the Pentecostal flame burn within my heart and mind so that I, too, may witness to you in eloquence, boldness, and accuracy.

Scott Hoezee

Lord, shall we not bring these gifts to Your service?
Shall we not bring to Your service all our powers
For life, for dignity, grace and order,

And intellectual pleasures of the senses?
The Lord who created must wish us to create
And employ our creation again in His service
Which is already His service in creating.

T. S. Eliot

To Music bent is my retired mind.
    And fain would I some song of pleasure sing,
But in vain joys no comfort now I find;
    From heavenly thoughts all true delight doth spring.
Thy power, O God, thy mercies, to record,
Will sweeten every note and every word.

All earthly pomp or beauty to express
    Is but to carve in snow, on waves to write.
Celestial things, though men conceive them less,
    Yet fullest are they in themselves of light;
Such beams they yield as know no means to die,
Such heat they cast as lifts the Spirit high.

Thomas Campion

From "Poem in the Rain and the Sun"

Sweet Christ, discover diamonds
And sapphires in my verse

While I burn the sap of my pine house
For the praise of the ocean sun!

I have walked upon the surf
Rinsing the bays with Thy hymns.
My prayers have swept the horizons clean
Of ships and rain.
All the waters are slick as lacquer.
Upon these polished swells my feet no longer run:
Sliding all over the waves I come
To the hope of a slippery harbor.

The dogs have gone back to their ghosts
And the many lions, home.
But words fling wide the windows of their glassy houses.

Then Adam and Eve come out and walk along the coast
Praising the tears of the sun
While I am decorating with Thy rubies the bones of the
    autumn trees,
The bones of the homecoming world.

Thomas Merton

Thou takest the pen — and the lines dance. Thou takest
the flute — and the notes shimmer. Thou takest the brush
and the colours sing. So all things have meaning and
beauty in that space beyond time where Thou art. How,
then, can I hold back anything from Thee?

Dag Hammarskjöld

Footnote to All Prayers

He whom I bow to only knows to whom I bow
When I attempt the ineffable Name, murmuring *thou,*
And dream of Pheidian fancies and embrace in heart
Symbols (I know) which cannot be the thing thou art.
Thus always, taken at their word, all prayers blaspheme
Worshipping with frail images a folk-lore dream,
And all men in their praying, self-deceived, address
The coinage of their own unquiet thoughts, unless
Thou, in magnetic mercy to thyself divert
Our arrows aimed unskillfully, beyond desert;
And all men are idolators, crying unheard
To a deaf idol, if thou take them at their word.

Take not, O Lord, our literal sense. Lord, in thy great
Unbroken speech our limping metaphor translate.

C. S. Lewis

My God, my God, Thou art a direct God. May I not say a literal God, a God that wouldst be understood literally and according to the plain sense of all that thou sayest?

But thou art also (Lord I intend it to thy glory, and let no profane misinterpreter abuse it to thy diminution), Thou art a figurative, a metaphorical God, too.

A God in whose words there is such a height of figures, such voyages, such peregrinations to fetch remote and precious metaphors, such extensions, such spreadings, such curtains of allegories, such third heavens of hyperboles, so harmonious elocutions, so retired and so reserved expressions, so commanding persuasions, so persuading commandments, such sinews even in thy milk, and such things in thy words, as all profane authors seem of the seed of the serpent that creeps, Thou art the Dove that flies.

O, what words but thine can express the inexpressible texture and composition of thy word, in which to one man that argument that binds his faith to believe that to be the word of God is the reverent simplicity of the word and to another the majesty of the word.

And in which two men equally pious may meet and one wonder that all should not understand it, and the other as much that any man should. . . .

Neither art thou thus a figurative, a metaphorical God in thy word only, but in thy works too. . . .

How often, how much more often, doth thy Son call himself a way, and a light, and a gate, and a vine, and bread than the Son of God or of man? How much oftener doth he exhibit a metaphorical Christ than a real, a literal?

This hath occasioned thine ancient servants . . . to proceed the same way in their expositions of the Scriptures and in their composing both of public liturgies and of private prayers to thee, to make their accesses to thee in such a kind of language as thou wast pleased to speak to them in a figurative, in a metaphorical language. . . .

As therefore the morning dew is a pawn [promise] of the evening fatness, so, O Lord, let this day's comfort be the earnest of tomorrow's, so far as may conform me entirely

to thee to what end and by what way soever Thy mercy
have appointed me.

John Donne

Eternal God,
whom our words may cradle but never contain,
we thank you for all the sound and silence
and color and symbol
which through the centuries have helped
the worship of your church
to be relevant and real.

A Wee Worship Book

All, absolutely all,
by your grace
speaks to me of you.

When I write
I ask
in your hands to be
the blank sheet of paper
where you can write what you please.

When I skim through a book
I feel acutely anxious
that such a lot of words should not go fruitless

THE WRITER ATTENDS TO THE WORD

and that no one should write
without some happy message for the world.

Every step I take
reminds me that,
wherever I am going,
I am always on the march to eternity.

The din of human life,
the dry leaves eddying on the ground,
the passing cars,
shop-windows full of goods,
the policeman on point-duty,
the milk-float,
the poor man begging,
the staircase and the lift,
the railway lines, the furrows of the sea,
the pedigree dog and the ownerless dog,
the pregnant woman,
the paper-boy,
the man who sweeps the streets,
the church, the school,
the office and the factory,
streets being widened,
hills being laid low,
the outward and the homeward road,
the key I use to open my front door;
whether sleeping or waking —
all, all, all
makes me think of you.
   What can I give to the Lord
   for all he has given to me?

Dom Helder Camara

You had no words at the Baptism, Mute Spirit:

Your assignments were
    to swoop and to settle —
        a fluttering image of
            pleasure and grace.

You had no speaking part in the garden,
    nor at cruel Golgotha.
        Three days later when the tomb burst open
            you remained silent.

Even in the Upper Room
    when you poured out a rampage of wind and fire:
    Even on that day when you powered tongues —
    cloven tongues of flame, other spoken tongues —
        you yourself, dear Spirit, acted without a script.

So I am not asking for words from you here.
    To hunt for them is my office and my obligation.
    One thing alone I seek from you —
        your brooding presence.

                                    Elizabeth Stickney

... Person
or, A Hymn on and to the Holy Ghost

How should I find speech
to you, the self-effacing

whose other self was seen
alone by the only one,

to you whose self-knowing
is perfect known to him,
seeing him only, loving
with him, yourself unseen?

Let the one you show me
ask you, for me,
you, all but lost in
the one in three,

to lead *my* self, effaced
in the known Light,
to be in him released
from facelessness,

so that where you
(unseen, unguessed, liable
to grievous hurt) would go
I may show him visible.

Margaret Avison

You asked for my hands,
that you might use them for your purpose.
I gave them for a moment, then withdrew them,
for the work was hard.
You asked for my mouth
to speak out against injustice.

I gave you a whisper that I might not be accused.
You asked for my eyes
to see the pain of poverty.
I closed them, for I did not want to see.
You asked for my life,
that you might work through me.
I gave a small part, that I might not get too involved.
Lord, forgive my calculated efforts to serve you —
only when it is convenient for me to do so,
only in those places where it is safe to do so,
and only with those who make it easy to do so.
Father, forgive me,
renew me, send me out
as a usable instrument,
that I might take seriously
the meaning of your cross. Amen.

Joe Seremane

Love Made Visible

An artist would sculpt or paint you
and make of you an image
worthy of a gaze
intent enough
to behold all of your
wonder in just one glance.

A poet would fashion you into
a sonnet or a cinquain,
an ode or a sestina,

or maybe a ghazal
with just enough words
to utter you in,
to proclaim you forth,
sweetly.

But I have only this work
here, day after day,
to attend
and out of this daily
drudgery must lift
tired hands
and pull you
out of sheer possibility,
a task so difficult that
some days
my open heart
gapes
and nothing but the swish of
the Spirit's breath moving through
me could ever energize this effort
enough to call it a masterpiece.

Beth Fritsch

The Ebb and Flow

When first thou on me Lord wrought'st Thy sweet print,
    My heart was made Thy tinder-box.
    My 'ffections were Thy tinder in't,
    Where fell Thy sparks by drops.

Those holy sparks of heavenly fire that came
    Did ever catch and often out would flame.

But now my heart is made Thy censer trim,
    Full of Thy golden altar's fire,
    To offer up sweet incense in
    Unto Thyself entire:
I find my tinder scarce Thy sparks can feel
That drop out from Thy holy flint and steel.

Hence doubts out bud for fear Thy fire in me
    'S a mocking ignis fatuus
    Or lest Thine altar's fire out be,
    It's hid in ashes thus.
Yet when the bellows of Thy spirit blow
Away mine ashes, then Thy fire doth glow.

Edward Taylor

A Lament

O Lord, I don't know what comes next. Am I past my
prime? Am I a sack of trinkets, emptied out? A once-
shimmering pool, evaporated? A spinner spun down,
tipped sidelong, stilled? Is this a drooping, dry, dissipating
drift toward some awful blank forever?

On some days, my work seemed a sweet sachet, crafted in
satin, scented with pungent words: "purpose," "calling." Or

a journey toward visioned destinations, worth all the ache and sweat.

But if this is only a rest, then why do I feel so restless and dull?

So much depends on the metaphor we choose for this — wouldn't you agree, my God? You are Lord of the freeze and the thaw, fullness and emptiness, purpose and wandering. Let's call me a tree, and this a winter — I'm all for cliché in a crisis. Let's say that shivery, barren days hunker us down to the deep. Tell me, God, to hold fast to the banks of the river. Tell me I will bear fruit in season. Show me the pale green at the root, the lively bulbs beneath the crusted loam, the small creatures curled in furry warmth. Tune me to the hushed inhale of promise, the stillness before chattering birds.

O Lord, do not forget. Let the seasons turn. Quicken me.

Debra Rienstra

My Lord, I have nothing to do in this World, but to seek
    and serve thee;
I have nothing to do with a Heart and its Affections but to
    breathe after thee.
I have nothing to do with my Tongue and Pen, but to
    speak to thee and for thee

and to publish thy Glory and thy Will. . . . What have I to
do with my remaining Time, even these last and
languishing hours, but to look up unto thee, and wait
for thy Grace, and thy Salvation?

Richard Baxter

Prayer for Utterance

Unless you build the house of this poem,
I who build it build it in vain. Unless
the words you give to me take part
in the word that is your Word,
I stray from my eternal home.
Unless your Spirit hover
on the face of my waters, they return
formless and void. What in me is dark
illumine. Not my will, but thine, O Lord,
as I face the cross of this day's page.
Before a word is on my tongue,
you know it, Lord, altogether.
You know each raftered part of me,
fitted together in the womb.
You know which way the ink will flow,
each start of hope, each rub of loss,
when all that I can do is groan.
Praise be to you, Author and Finisher.
Praise of morning be to you.

Paul Willis

The Writer Finds Joy in the Work

There be many that say, Who will show us any good? LORD, lift thou up the light of thy countenance upon us. Thou has put gladness in my heart, more than in the time that their corn and their wine increased.

PSALM 4.6-7

When Gustav Flaubert, the writer of perhaps the greatest psychological novel ever written, once considered the nature of the writer's life, he was direct and clear: Writing, he wrote, "is a dog's life."

Gather together a group of writers and you will soon hear of the ways and means of procrastination, of the modes of postponement, of the tyranny of the blank page, troubles with character, setting, plot, diction, tone, the beads of frustration that are the writer's constant companions. More viscerally, writers compare writing to opening a vein and letting blood flow over the keys. They use words like "terror," "hard work," "writer's block." They confess to wondering if they can ever finish a project — or if they ever will have another project.

So.

The obvious question here is, Why put yourself through this agony?

And here, writers use other words. Maurice Sendak speaks of the release of the creative urge. Theodore Roosevelt, surprisingly America's most published president, speaks of the pleasure of seeing a stack of pages piling up on his desk. Writers use words like "relief," "fulfillment," "sense of completion," insight," "illumination," and even "delight."

J. R. R. Tolkien referred to humanity as "sub-creators," those who are created to create. Perhaps much of the delight of writing comes from accomplishing what we are meant to accomplish: to create. Perhaps much of the delight of writing comes from the reaching through the hard work and terror and bloody keyboard. Perhaps much of the delight of writing comes from a recognition that skills, used well, are pleasing in the use and in the culmination — and in the sharing.

There are times in the writer's life when the writing seems like a gift. An idea, a pattern, a structure, a sentence, a phrase, a word that comes to us unexpectedly, mysteriously, seemingly un-earned, perhaps providential. This may happen at the typewriter, or at the laundry, or driving hungry hordes back from school to-ward chocolate chip cookies and milk, or standing on the side-lines at a Saturday morning soccer game. We had not expected it; we had not even been working at it. And yet there the thing is, and the pleasure of its sudden appearance is the pleasure of true hope.

There are times in the reader's life that the writing seems in-evitable. Of course this must be the next word. Of course this must be the next sentence. Of course this image must blossom into this set of ideas. Of course, of course. But writing is never in-evitable. The writer chooses from a small infinity of words each time she sets one down. It is the craft of the writer that has prompted the illusion of inevitability for the reader.

In these, the writer, the sub-creator, shows delight — creating what, it seems, he or she must create, in just the way it must be created. What else could there be but delight, when craft, gift, skill, learning, intent, beauty, and meaning buckle?

How easy for me to live with you, Lord!
How easy to believe in you!
When my mind casts about
Or flags in bewilderment,
when the cleverest among us
cannot see past the present evening,
not knowing what to do tomorrow —
you send me the clarity to know
that you exist
and will take care
that not all paths of goodness shall be barred.
At the crest of earthly fame
I look back in wonderment
at the journey beyond hope — to this place,
from which I was able to send mankind
a reflection of your rays.
And however long the time
that I must yet reflect them
you will give it me.
And whatever I fail to accomplish
you surely have allotted unto others.

Aleksandr Solzhenitsyn

God, who wrestled with chaos to create matter, and over-came death to bring us to eternal life, give to writers, musicians and artists a share in the work and joy of creation, that, like you, they may draw forth beauty out of nothingness, and reveal to us some glimpses of your eternity, where you are enthroned, Life-giver, Pain-bearer, Love-maker, alive for ever and ever.

Michael John Radford Counsell

Thank you, O God, for all the help you have given me
    today.
Thank you for
Keeping me safe all through today;
Helping me to do my work through today;
Giving me strength to conquer my temptations all through
    today.
Thank you for
My home and all that it has been to me;
My loved ones and all the circle of those most dear;
My friends and comrades with whom I have worked and
    talked.
Thank you for
Any kindness I have received;
Any help that was given to me;

Any sympathy that was shown to me.

Help me to lay myself down to sleep tonight, with a glad
and grateful heart.

This I ask through Jesus Christ my Lord. Amen.

William Barclay

How could anything rightly be said about love if Thou
wert forgotten, Thou God of love, from whom all love
comes in heaven and on earth; Thou who didst hold nothing back but didst give everything in love; Thou who art
love, so the lover is only what he is through being in Thee!
How could anything rightly be said about love if Thou
wert forgotten, Thou who didst make manifest what love
is, Thou, our Savior and Redeemer, who gave Himself to
save us all! How could anything rightly be said about love
if Thou wert forgotten, Thou spirit of love, Thou who dost
abate nothing of Thine own, but dost call to mind the sacrifice of love, dost remind the believer to love as he is
loved, and his neighbor as himself! O eternal love! Thou
who art everywhere present, and never without testimony
in what may here be said about love, or about works of
love. For it is certainly true that there are some acts which
the human language particularly and narrow-mindedly
calls acts of charity; but in heaven it is certainly true that
no act can be pleasing unless it is an act of love: sincere in
its self-abnegation, a necessity for love, and just because of
this, without claim or merit.

Søren Kierkegaard

Dear Artist of the Universe, Beloved Sculptor, Singer, and
Author of my life, born of your image I have made a home
in the open fields of your heart. The magnetic tug of your
invitation to grow is slowly transforming me into a gift for
the world. Mentor me into healthy ways of living.

Macrina Wiederkehr

Beauty

Christ, keep me from the self-survey
    Of beauties all Thine own;
If there is beauty, let me pray,
    And praise the Lord alone.

Pray — that I may the fiend withstand,
    Where'er his serpents be;
Praise — that the Lord's almighty hand
    Is manifest in me.

It is not so — my features are
    Much meaner than the rest;
A glow-worm cannot be a star,
    And I am plain at best.

Then come, my Love, Thy grace impart,
    Great Savior of mankind;

O come and purify my heart
   And beautify my mind.

Then will I Thy carnations nurse
   And cherish every rose,
And empty to the poor my Purse
   Till grace to glory grows.

Christopher Smart

O Christ who holds
the open gate,
O Christ who drives the furrow straight,
O Christ, the plow, O Christ, the laughter
Of holy white birds flying after,
Lo, all my heart's field red and torn,
And thou wilt bring the young green corn,
The young green corn for ever singing;
And when the field is fresh and fair
Thy blessed feet shall glitter there.
And we will walk the weeded field,
And tell the golden harvest's yield,
The corn that makes the holy bread
By which the soul of man is fed,
The holy bread, the food unpriced,
Thy everlasting mercy, Christ.

John Masefield

Shine forth, O Lord . . . let Thy glory blossom forth as bloom and foliage on the trees; change with Thy mighty power this visible world into that diviner world, which as yet we see not; destroy what we see, that it may pass and be transformed into what we believe. Bright as is the sun, and the sky, and the clouds; green as are the leaves and the fields; sweet as is the singing of the birds; we know that they are not all, and we will not take up with a part for the whole. They proceed from a centre of love and goodness, which is God Himself; but they are not His fullness; they speak of heaven, but they are not heaven; they are but as stray beams and dim reflections of His Image; they are but crumbs from the table. We are looking for the coming of the day of God. . . .

John Henry Newman

You see, I want a lot.
Maybe I want it all:
The darkness of each endless fall,
The shimmering light of each ascent.

So many are alive who don't seem to care.
Casual, easy, they move in the world
As though untouched.

But you take pleasure in the faces
Of those who know they thirst.

You cherish those
Who grip you for survival.

You are not dead yet, it's not too late
To open your depths by plunging into them
And drink in the life
That reveals itself quietly there.

Rainer Maria Rilke

To Jesus on Easter

You see the universe, as I see daylight
opening to Your heart
like fingers of a little child uncurling.

It lies to You no more than wood to blade,
nor will You tell me lies.
Only fools or cowards lie. And You are neither.

Not that I comprehend You, who are simpler
than all our words about You,
and deeper. They drop around You like dead leaves.

Yet I can trust You. You resembling me —
two eyes, two hands, two feet,
five senses and no more — will cup my being,

spilling toward nothingness, within Your palm.
And when the last bridge breaks,
I shall walk on the bright span of Your breath.

Vassar Miller

Make of me a twilight: wake of color, trail of glory. In the
evening of life transform me into a song of gratitude. I want
to be an evening star for those who have lost their way. I
want to be beauty at the end of each day. On my pilgrimage
through the day, write mystery stories with my life.

Macrina Wiederkehr

Creator God,
because you make all that draws forth our praise
and the forms in which to express it,
we praise you.
Because you make artists of us all,
awakening courage to look again at what is taken for
    granted,
grace to share these insights with others,
vision to reveal the future already in being,
we praise you.
Because you form your Word among us,
and in your great work embrace all human experience,
even death itself, inspiring our resurrection song,
we praise you.
Yours is the glory.

Douglas Galbraith

I'll praise my Maker while I've breath;
And when my voice is lost in death,
Praise shall employ my nobler powers:
My days of praise shall ne'er be past
While life, and thought, and being last
Or immortality endures.

Isaac Watts

You, Creator God, called all things into being.
   And you named the great spaces:
      light
      darkness
      heavens
      earth
      sea

You gave to humans the delight and the duty of naming
   All those things that crowd into our days:
      cats and spiders
      lovers and friends
      daffodils and muskrats
      slimy ponds and dead leaves
      sorrow and joy.

We thank you for writers who wake us up,
   Who call us to attention;

We thank you for authors who craft words
That reverberate in our ears and in our hearts.

We thank you for the Word made flesh
for the Spirit who moves in and among us
for the lovingkindness of our heavenly Father.

All this we pray through the power of the Holy Spirit,
And in the name of Christ Jesus our Lord.

Susan Felch

For this fine-tipped pen my fingers cradle,
For newly-sharpened yellow pencils,
For the home-made notebook,
The reams of computer paper —
praise.

For pink erasers,
For the rainbow of sticky notes,
The printer ink,
The typewriter ribbon (hoarded and cherished) —
praise.

For library stacks,
For the bookstore café
The study carrel,
The ample desk —
praise.

For the cloud of witnesses ranged on the bookshelves,
For the challenge of an empty page,

For the dream that awakens me,
The faith that persists after the rejection letter,
The hope I slide into a new manila envelope
The joy you give me through this work —
praise.

For the grand symphony of language,
For the hardware of grammar,
For the infinite palette of words,
The game of it all,
This bounteous feast —
praise, all praise.

Elizabeth Stickney

The Prayer of the Author

Grant, I beseech Thee,
that all who read this book may be conscious of the deep
spiritual insight of the writer;
that the sale of this book may result in a nice little nest-
egg, even after income tax has been deducted;
that copies of this book, nicely bound, may make an
impressive sight in the study, on the bookshelf which
is level with the eye;
that amid all the congratulatory applause, the writer may
remain conspicuously humble.

David Head

Here, O Lord, is my poor heart,
an empty vessel ready to be filled with your grace.
Here, O Lord, is my sinful soul,
waiting to be refreshed by your love.
Here, O Lord, is my mouth
created for your praise and ready to proclaim
the glory of your name,
now and for ever.

Dwight Lyman Moody

And now, I beseech thee, good Jesus, that to whom thou
hast graciously granted sweetly to partake of the words of
thy wisdom and knowledge, thou wilt also vouchsafe that
he may some time or other come to thee, the fountain of
all wisdom, and always appear before thy face, who livest
and reignest world without end.

The Venerable Bede

Jesus, the very thought of Thee
With sweetness fills my breast;
But sweeter far Thy face to see,
And in Thy presence rest.

No voice can sing, no heart can frame,
Or can the memory find
A sweeter sound than Jesus' name,
O Savior of mankind.

O Hope of every contrite heart!
O Joy of all the meek!
To those who fall, how kind thou art!
How good to those who seek!

But what to those who find? Ah! This,
No tongue or pen can show
The love of Jesus, what it is
None but His loved ones know.

Bernard of Clairvaux

"You are drunk, but not with wine"
ISAIAH 51.21

O God of too much giving, whence is this
inebriation that possesses me,
that the staid road now wanders all amiss
and that the wind walks much too giddily,
clutching a bush for balance, or a tree?
How then can dignity and pride endure
with such inordinate mirth upon the land,
when steps and speech are somewhat insecure
and the light heart is wholly out of hand?

If there be indecorum in my songs,
fasten the blame where rightly it belongs:
on him who offered me too many cups
of his most potent goodness — not on me,
a peasant who, because a King was host,
drank out of courtesy.

Jessica Powers

7

The Writer Petitions

Give ear to my prayer, O God; and hide not thyself from my supplication. Attend unto me, and hear me.

PSALM 55.1-2A

There is an old Hasidic tale of a rabbi — Who knows his name? — who lives alone — Who knows where? — and who prays one prayer and only one prayer each morning: "Lord, let the world continue to be for one more day." That is his prayer. And, the tale says, if the rabbi should, one day, fail to utter the prayer — if he should miss the time, or fall, or forget — and the prayer is not uttered, then the world will cease to exist.

Things are that tenuous.

For writers, their work is prayer.

In writing, the writer offers order, and beauty, and meaning, and insight. In writing, the writer holds up art against a spinning world and its darkness, against its fractures, against its chaos and anger and brokenness. In writing, the author holds up this prayer: "Lord, let the world continue to be for one more day."

Aristotle speaks to the role of art as recognition, the sense that in the piece, the reader somehow sees herself, or the world around her. The writer, somehow, no matter how distant it is in time and space, leads the reader to say, "Ah, that is me." There is, of course, a fearful suggestion in this, because that recognition might lead the reader to truths that are hard and painful to confront. But is there not, too, the sense that the reader can, in recognition, know that he is not alone in the world, that others have seen what he has seen, and know what he has known, and suffered what he has suffered? Is it not, too, the case that the reader can, in a world of easy cynicism, see that others have passed through what she is passing through and found — surprise! — that the world is most worthy the winning?

Lord, let the world continue to be for one more day.

Certainly it may be that the writer asks, in prayer, for the right word, the right image. Perhaps the writer asks for the time and opportunity to craft what is in her heart. Perhaps the writer asks for that one editor who has a sense of the writer's purpose and intent, that editor who will help bring it all to fruition.

But beneath all of those prayers is the deeper one: that the writer's art might hold the darkness and chaos at bay. That the writer's art can somehow — Who knows how? — help the world continue to be, at least for one more reader, for one more day.

Lord, teach us to pray. Some of us are not skilled in the art of prayer. As we draw near to Thee in thought, our spirits long for Thy Spirit, and reach out for Thee, longing to feel Thee near. We know not how to express the deepest emotions that lie hidden in our hearts.

In these moments, we have no polished phrases with which to impress one another, no finely molded, delicately turned clauses to present to Thee. Nor would we be confined to conventional petitions and repeat our prayers like the unwinding of a much-exposed film. We know, our Father, that we are praying most when we are saying least. We know that we are closest to Thee when we have left behind the things that have held us captive so long. . . .

We thank Thee that Thou are hearing us even now. We thank Thee for the grace of prayer. We thank Thee for Thyself.

Peter Marshall

But O Thou, the Merciful Father of Spirits, the Attractive of Love, and Ocean of Delights. . . . O keep me while I tarry on this Earth, in daily serious breathings after Thee, and in a believing, affectionate walking with Thee: And when Thou comest, O let me be found so doing; not hiding my Talent, not serving my Flesh, nor yet asleep with my Lamp unfurnished; but waiting and longing for my Lord's return. That those who shall reade these heavenly Directions, may not reade only the fruit of my Studies, and the product of my fancy, but the breathings of my active Hope and Love: That if my heart were open to their view, they might there reade the same most deeply engraven, with a Beam from the face of the Sonne of God; and not find Vanity, or Lust, or Pride within, where the words of Life appear without; that so these lines may not witness against me; but proceeding from the heart of the writer, may be effectuall through Thy grace upon the heart of the Reader; and so be the savour of Life to both.

Richard Baxter

Many, O Lord, are the wonderful works which you have wrought. They cannot be reckoned up in order. If we should declare and speak of them, they are more than we can number. We give praise for the creation of the world, for the majesty of the mountains and for the mighty deeps, for the myriad number of all your creatures, each sustaining its life according to the plan you have ordained. We give praise for the life of man, whom you have created in your image and called into fellowship with you, whom you have endowed with memory and foresight, so that all our yesterdays are gathered together in our present moment and all our tomorrows are the objects of our hopes and apprehensions.

O Lord, you have made us very great. Help us to remember how weak we are, so that we may not deny our kinship with the creatures of the field and our common dependence with them upon summer and winter, day and night. O Lord, you have made us very small, and we bring our years to an end like a tale that is told; help us to remember that beyond our brief day is the eternity of your love.

Reinhold Niebuhr

Lemuel's Blessing

Let my ignorance and my failings
Remain far behind me like tracks made in a wet season,
At the end of which I have vanished,
So that those who track me for their own twisted ends
May be rewarded only with ignorance and failings.
But let me leave my cry stretched out behind me like a
    road
On which I have followed you.
And sustain me for my time in the desert
On what is essential to me.

W. S. Merwin

Give us grace Almighty Father so to pray as to deserve to be heard, to address Thee with our hearts, as with our lips. Thou are every where present, from Thee no secret can be hid. May the knowledge of this teach us to fix our thoughts on Thee, with reverence and devotion that we pray not in vain.

Jane Austen

Keep us Lord so awake in the duties of our callings that we may thus sleep in thy peace, and wake in thy glory, and change that infallibility which thou affordest us here, to an actual and undeterminable possession of that kingdom which thy Son our Saviour Jesus Christ hath purchased for us.

John Donne

For Those Whose Work Is Invisible

For those who paint the undersides of boats,
Makers of ornamental drains on roofs — too high to be
    seen,
Cobblers who labor over inner soles,

Seamstresses who stitch the wrong sides of linings,
For scholars whose research leads to no obvious discovery,
For dentists who polish each gold surface of the fillings of
    upper molars,
For civil engineers and those who repair water mains,
For electricians, for artists who suppress what does
    injustice to their visions,
For surgeons whose sutures are things of beauty.
For all those whose work is for Your eye only,
Who labor for Your entertainment or their own,
Who sleep in peace or do not sleep in peace, knowing their
    efforts are unknown.
Protect them from downheartedness — and from diseases
    of the eye.
Grant them perseverance, for the sake of Your love, which
    is humble, invisible and heedless of reward.

Mary Gordon

O God, who hast hitherto supported me, enable me to proceed in this labour, and in the Whole task of my present
state; that when I shall render up, at the last day, an ac-
count of the talent committed to me, I may receive pardon,
for the sake of Jesus Christ.

Samuel Johnson

Prosper thou the works of my hands, O Lord;
O, prosper thou my handy-work.

Thomas Ken

Dear Lord, you have sent me into this world to preach
your word. So often the problems of the world seem so
complex and intricate that your word strikes me as embar-
rassingly simple. Many times I feel tongue-tied in the
company of people who are dealing with the world's social
and economic problems. But you, O Lord, said, "Be clever
as serpents and innocent as doves." Let me retain inno-
cence and simplicity in the midst of this complex world. I
realize that I have to be informed, that I have to study the
many aspects of the problems facing the world, and that I
have to try to understand as well as possible the dynamics
of our contemporary society. But what really counts is that
all this information, knowledge, and insight allows me to
speak more clearly and unambiguously your truthful
word. Do not allow evil powers to seduce me with the
complexities of the world's problems. But give me strength
to think clearly, speak freely, and act boldly in your service. Give me the courage to show the dove in a world so
full of serpents.

Henri Nouwen

O Lord Jesus Christ, the I AM, cast down, I beseech Thee, before the unapproachable Majesty of Thy Being, all man's haughtiness of will and pride of intellect. Make the wise and prudent of this world as babes, that they may desire the sincere milk of Thy Word: Let them not wrest Thy good gifts to their own destruction, but with great abilities and great responsibilities bestow, O Lord, our Wisdom, greater grace.

Christina Rossetti

O Word Made Flesh, stand at the gate of my mouth. Be my voice this day that the words I speak will be healing, affirming, true, and gentle. Give me wisdom to think before I speak. Bless the words in me that are waiting to be spoken. Live and abide in my words so that others will feel safe in my presence. Surprise me with words that have come from you. Oh, place my words in the kiln of your heart that they may be enduring and strong, tempered and seasoned with love and resilience. Give me a well-trained tongue that has been borne out of silent listening in the sanctuary of my heart. May my words become love in the lives of others.

Macrina Wiederkehr

Creator Spirit, by whose aid
The world's foundations first were laid,
Come visit ev'ry pious mind;
Come pour thy joys on humankind:
From sin and sorrow set us free;
And make thy temples worthy thee.
O, source of uncreated light,
The Father's promised Paraclete!
Thrice holy fount, thrice holy fire,
Our hearts with heav'nly love inspire;
Come, and thy sacred unction bring
To sanctify us, while we sing!
Plenteous of grace, descend from high,
Rich in thy sev'n-fold energy!
Thou strength of his almighty hand,
Whose pow'r does heav'n and earth command:
Proceeding Spirit, our defence,
Who dost the gift of tongues dispense,
And crown'st thy gift, with eloquence!
Refine and purge our earthy parts;
But, oh, inflame and fire our hearts!
Our frailties help, our vice control;
Submit the senses to the soul;
And when rebellious they are grown,
Then, lay thy hand, and hold 'em down.
Chase from our minds th'infernal foe;
And peace, the fruit of love, bestow:
And, lest our feet should step astray,
Protect, and guide us in the way.

Make us eternal truths receive,
And practice all that we believe:
Give us thy self, that we may see
The Father and the Son, by thee.
Immortal honour, endless fame
Attend th'almighty Father's name:
The saviour Son be glorified,
Who for lost man's redemption died:
And equal adoration be
Eternal Paraclete, to thee.

John Dryden, translator

Lord God, we have given more weight to our successes
　　and our happiness than to your will.
We have eaten without a thought for the hungry.
We have spoken without an effort to understand others.
We have kept silence instead of telling the truth.
We have judged others, forgetful that you alone are the
　　Judge.
We have acted rather in accordance with our opinions
　　than according to your commands.
Within your church we have been slow to practice love of
　　our neighbors.
And in the world we have not been your faithful servants.
Forgive us and help us to live as disciples of Jesus Christ,
　　Your Son, our Savior. Amen.

Conference of European Churches

O Lord, open my eyes
that I may see the need of others,
open my ears that I may hear their cries,
open my heart so that they need not be without succour.
Let me not be afraid to defend the weak
because of the anger of the strong,
nor afraid to defend the poor
because of the anger of the rich.
Show me where love and hope and faith are needed,
and use me to bring them to these places.
Open my eyes and ears that I may, this coming day,
be able to do some work of peace for thee.

Alan Paton

He who would be great among you

You whose birth broke all the
social & biological rules —
son of the poor who accepted
the worship due a king —
child prodigy debating with
the Temple Th.D.s — you
were the kind who used
a new math
to multiply bread, fish, faith.

You practiced a
radical sociology:
rehabilitated con men &
call girls. You valued women
& other minority groups.
A G.P., you specialized in
heart transplants.
Creator, healer,
shepherd, innovator,
story-teller, weather-maker,
botanist, alchemist,
exorcist, iconoclast,
seeker, seer, motive-sifter,
you were always beyond,
above us. Ahead
of your time, & ours.

And we would like
to be *like* you. Bold
as Boanerges, we hear ourselves
demand: "Admit us
to your avant-garde.
Grant us a degree
in all the liberal arts
of heaven."
Why our belligerence?
Why does this whiff of fame
and greatness smell so sweet?
Why must we compete
to be first? Have we forgotten
how you took, simply, cool water
and a towel for our feet?

Luci Shaw

The Doubter's Prayer

While faith is with me, I am best;
It turns my darkest night to day;
But, while I clasp it to my breast,
I often feel it slide away. . . .

What shall I do if all my love,
My hopes, my toil, are cast away?
And if there be no God above
To hear and bless me when I pray?

Oh, help me, God! For thou alone
Canst my distracted soul relieve.
Forsake it not: it is thine own,
Though weak, yet longing to believe.

Anne Brontë

You needed no help from us, Lord, and yet you made us
to be namers, to be interpreters, to be tellers of stories, to
be weavers of culture. In all of this we shadow your Word
in the on-going work of creation. And because of all this
we stand in awe and praise you.

We ask that you help us to see, to notice, to be responsive to your leadings in our lives.

We ask that you help us relish the well-chosen word,

the well-wrought sentence, and the wonder of meeting others' minds.

We ask that you grant us peace and patience in the revision associated with work on this side of perfection.

We ask that you nourish our hope that we too might bring splendor into your new city.

And we ask that you help us never to forget that the only way we in ourselves will live forever is not through our work but through having our names engraved on your palms.

In your name, the name above all names, we pray.

William J. Vande Kopple

And give me Good Lord, an humble, lowly, quyet, peaceable, pacyent, charitable, kinde, tender, and pytyfull mynde, with all my workes and all my words and all my thoughts, to have a taste of thy blessed Holy Spyrite.

Sir Thomas More

Lord, help us to remember what we do not know and to know what we remember to be true.

Donald R. Hettinga

Shall the Dead Praise Thee?

I cannot praise Thee. By his instrument
    The master sits, and moves nor foot nor hand;
For see the organ pipes, this, that way bent,
    Leaning, o'erthrown, like wheat-stalks tempest fanned!

I well could praise Thee for a flower, a dove,
    But not for Life that is not life in me;
Nor for a being that is less than Love —
    A barren shoal half lifted from a sea.

Unto a land where no wind bloweth ships
    Thy Wind one day will blow me to my own:
Rather I'd kiss no more their loving lips
    Than carry them a heart so poor and prone.

I bless Thee, Father, Thou art what Thou art,
    That Thou dost know Thyself what Thou dost know —
A perfect, simple, tender, rhythmic heart,
    Beating its blood to all in bounteous flow.

And I can bless Thee too for every smart,
    For every disappointment, ache, and fear;
For every hook Thou fixest in my heart,
    For every burning cord that draws me near.

But prayer these wake, not song. Thyself I crave.
    Come Thou, or all Thy gifts away I fling.
Thou silent, I am but an empty grave:
    Think to me, Father, and I am a king!

My organ pipes will then stand up awake,
    Their life soar, as from smoldering wood the blaze;
And swift contending harmonies shall shake
    Thy windows with a storm of jubilant praise.

George MacDonald

The Elixir

    Teach me, my God and King,
    In all things thee to see,
And what I do in anything,
    To do it as for thee:

    Not rudely, as a beast,
    To run into an action;
But still to make thee prepossessed,
    And give it his perfection.

    A man that looks on glass,
    On it may stay his eye;
Or if he pleaseth, through it pass,
    And then the heav'n espy.

    All may of thee partake:
    Nothing can be so mean,
Which with his tincture (for thy sake)
    Will not grow bright and clean.

    A servant with this clause
    Makes drudgery divine:

Who sweeps a room, as for thy laws,
    Makes that and th' action fine.

    This is the famous stone
    That turneth all to gold:
For that which God doth touch and own
    Cannot for less be told.

George Herbert

This Writer's Plea

Father God,
Am I sinful to request that my novel gets published?
    Picked up and published for others to read?
After all, you know our needs before we ask.
Perhaps my asking suggests a craving
beyond what is due, what is deserved.

Your Words declare that you won't deny good things to
    those who walk along your path.
Help me to believe this is a path designed by you.
Help me to see that you often allow us refreshment on our
    journey — a loving spouse, a sweet child, a satisfying
    job, a novel filled with words — and that we are not
    selfish when we don't want to let those gifts go.
And though the waiting continues and the answer is
    delayed, help me to trust that my writing — these
    words — are, indeed, from the giver of all good
    things who always finishes what He began.

Nancy Hull

Gratefulness

Thou that hast giv'n so much to me,
Give one thing more, a grateful heart.
See how thy beggar works on thee
      By art.

He makes thy gifts occasion more,
And says, If he in this be cross'd,
All thou hast giv'n him heretofore
      Is lost.

But thou didst reckon, when at first
Thy word our hearts and hands did crave,
What it would come to at the worst
      To save.

Perpetual knockings at thy door,
Tears sullying thy transparent rooms,
Gift upon gift, much would have more,
      And comes.

This not withstanding, thou wentst on,
And didst allow us all our noise:
Nay, thou hast made a sigh and groan
      Thy joys.

Not that thou hast not still above
Much better tunes, than groans can make;
But that these country airs thy love
      Did take.

Wherefore I cry, and cry again;
And in no quiet canst thou be,
Till I a thankful heart obtain
            Of thee:

Not thankful, when it pleaseth me;
As if thy blessings had spare days:
But such a heart, whose pulse may be
            Thy praise.

George Herbert

Prayer and Meditation for "A Girl Named Mister"

Thank you, Lord
for the gift of yourself as Word.
Thank you, Lord
for the gift to wield and weave the word.
Thank you, Lord
for the magic and the mystery,
and the power of word.

Lord, you are the first Author.
Please help me to write in a way
that is organic.
Guide my hand, my thoughts
to make your presence
in the world of my characters
as natural and necessary as breathing.

Lord, you knew and know Mary
as intimately
as you know and have known me.
Help me to climb
into her skin
and see the world
through her eyes.

Nikki Grimes

Spirit of God,
you are the breath of creation,
the wind of change that blows through our lives,
opening us up to new dreams and new hopes,
new life in Jesus Christ.
Forgive us our closed minds,
which barricade themselves against new ideas,
preferring the past
to what you might want to do through us tomorrow.
Forgive our closed eyes,
which fail to see the needs of your world,
blind to opportunities of service and love.
Forgive our closed hands,
which clutch our gifts and our wealth for our own use
    alone.
Forgive us our closed hearts,
Which limit our affections to ourselves and our own.
Spirit of new life,
forgive us and break down the prison walls of our
    selfishness,

that we might be open to your love
and open for service in your world,
Through Jesus Christ, our Lord.

Christopher Ellis

The Apologist's Evening Prayer

From all my lame defeats and oh! much more
From all the victories that I seemed to score;
From cleverness shot forth on Thy behalf
At which, while angels weep, the audience laugh;
From all my proofs of Thy divinity,
Thou, who wouldst give no sign, deliver me.

Thoughts are but coins. Let me not trust, instead
Of Thee, their thin-worn image of Thy head.
From all my thoughts, even from my thoughts of Thee,
O thou fair Silence, fall, and set me free.
Lord of the narrow gate and the needle's eye,
Take from me all my trumpery lest I die.

C. S. Lewis

May I be found worthy to do it! Lord, make me crystal
clear for Thy light to shine through.

Katherine Mansfield

8

The Writer Offers the Work to God

Praise ye the Lord; 'tis good to raise
Our hearts and voices in his praise;
His nature and his works invite
To make this duty our delight.

ISAAC WATTS
(PARAPHRASE OF PSALM 147)

Norwich Cathedral is famous for, among other architectural wonders, its roof bosses — small carved vignettes of Biblical scenes set where the ribbing of the vaults comes together. The scenes are from both the Old and New Testaments — the creation of Eve, Noah's Ark, Christ's ascension. They are intricately carved, with expressioned faces, textured clothing, defined features — and still they have the remnants of the bright paint that adorned them when first painted six centuries ago.

The sculptors are anonymous. We will never know the names of those who carved them.

And many of the bosses are completely inaccessible, given their height, to those standing on the floor below. If you go to Norwich Cathedral, you will stand on the floor and look straight up, and hardly be able to see them.

But six centuries ago, an artist carved these, and fastened them to the ceiling, and then turned his face from them and climbed down the scaffolding, and left his art for God.

"Go, little book," wrote Chaucer, and sent his writing out into the big wide world. For the last act of the writer is not to put his work into a file cabinet and slide the drawer closed; it is to send the pages out into the world, where, most certainly, the writer will not see all the effects those pages may have. Most of the readers who will come to it will be utterly unknown to the writer. Perhaps those pages might be misunderstood. And perhaps those pages may lead someone to a new awareness. "When the words mean even more than the writer knew they meant," Madeleine L'Engle writes, "then the writer has been listening. And sometimes when we listen, we are led into places we do not expect, into adventures we do not always understand."

Go, little book, and the writer climbs down from the scaffold with a smile, and a shudder.

The writer, like the sculptor at Norwich Cathedral, offers his

THE WRITER OFFERS THE WORK TO GOD

work up. Will he be remembered for it? Will it be seen? The sculptor, the writer, does not know.

All artists are vulnerable. Suppose there is no audience? Suppose no one will read or care about what you have given out of your heart's blood? Suppose the reviewers are brutal in their clever misunderstandings?

Suppose that the words are unacceptable after all?

It makes no difference. The writer is called to offer.

It is the offering that matters.

For the times I've made my writing my idol —
  Good Lord, forgive me.
For the times I expected those whom I love to bow down
    to my idol —
  Good Lord, forgive me.
For my vexations when people would not bow down and
    worship my idol,
    by interrupting me when I am writing,
    by valuing my writing less than I do,
    by becoming upset when my writing takes precedence
      over our common and and necessary labors,
    by refusing to serve art as I serve art;
    by refusing to serve me, the artist;
    by refusing to obey the commandments which my art-
      idol requires of everyone near to me —
  Good Lord, forgive me.
For the times when I have forgotten to thank you for
    having granted me the ability to write,
    or to praise you for the vocation —
  Good Lord, forgive me.
Because you have remembered me,
    I praise you, good Lord.
Because your Holy Spirit continues to breathe thought and
    words and purpose and goodness into my work,
    I praise you, good Lord.

Because you do forgive me, and because you are my God
  forever,
  I praise you, good Lord.

Walter Wangerin, Jr.

Stir us up to offer to Thee, O Lord, our bodies, our souls,
  our spirits,
in all we love and all we learn, in all we plan and all we
  do,
to offer our labours, our pleasures, our sorrows, to Thee;
to work for Thy kingdom through them,
to live as those who are not their own,
but bought with Thy blood, fed with Thy body. . . .
Thine from our birth-hour, Thine now, and Thine for ever.

Charles Kingsley

How shall I sing that majesty
Which angels do admire?
Let dust in dust and silence lie;
Sing, sing, ye heavenly choir.
Thousands of thousands stand around
Thy throne, O God most high;
Ten thousand times ten thousand sound
Thy praise; but who am I?

Thy brightness unto them appears,
Whilst I thy footsteps trace;
A sound of God comes to my ears,
But they behold thy face.
They sing because thou art their song;
Lord, send a beam on me;
For where heaven is but once begun
There alleluias be.

Enlighten with faith's light my heart,
Inflame it with love's fire;
Then shall I sing and bear a part
With that celestial choir.
I shall, I fear, be dark and cold,
With all my fire and light;
Yet when thou dost accept their gold,
Lord, treasure up my mite.

How great a being, Lord, is thine,
Which doth all beings keep!
Thy knowledge is the only line
To sound so vast a deep.
Thou art a sea without a shore,
A sun without a sphere;
Thy time is now and evermore,
Thy place is everywhere.

John Mason

Lord, teach us how to pray aright
With reverence and with fear;
Though dust and ashes in thy sight,
We may, we must, draw near.

We perish if we cease from prayer:
O grant us power to pray
And, when to meet thee we prepare,
Lord, meet us by the way.

God of all grace, we bring to thee
A broken, contrite heart;
Give what thine eye delights to see,
Truth in the inward part;

Faith in the only Sacrifice
That can for sin atone,
To cast our hopes, to fix our eyes,
On Christ, on Christ alone;

Patience to watch and wait and weep,
Though mercy long delay.
Courage our fainting souls to keep,
And trust thee though thou slay.

Give these, and then thy will be done;
Thus, strengthened with all might,
We, through thy Spirit and thy Son,
Shall pray, and pray aright.

James Montgomery

And so all men run after time, Lord.
They pass through life running —
Hurried, jostled, overburdened, frantic, and they never get
    there.
They haven't time.
In spite of all their efforts they're still short of time,
Of a great deal of time.
Lord, you must have made a mistake in your calculations.
There is a big mistake somewhere.
The hours are too short,
The days are too short,
Our lives are too short.
You who are beyond time, Lord, you smile to see us
    fighting it.
And you know what you are doing.
You make no mistakes in your distribution of time to
    men.
You give each one time to do what you want him to do.

But we must not lose time
Waste time,
Kill time,
For time is a gift that you give us,
But a perishable gift,
A gift that does not keep.

Lord, I have time,
I have plenty of time,
All the time that you give me,
The years of my life,

The days of my years,
The hours of my days,
They are all mine.
Mine to fill, quietly, calmly,
But to fill completely, up to the brim,
To offer them to you, that of their insipid water
You may make a rich wine
Such as you made once in Cana of Galilee.

I am not asking you tonight, Lord,
For time to do this and then that,
But your grace to do conscientiously,
In the time that you give me, what you want me to do.

Michael Quoist

King of glory, King of Peace,
   I will love thee;
And that love may never cease,
   I will move thee.

Thou hast granted my request,
   Thou hast heard me:
Thou dids't note my working breast,
   Thou hast spared me.

Wherefore with my utmost art
   I will sing thee,
And the cream of all my heart
   I will bring thee.

Though my sins against me cried,
    Thou didst clear me;
And alone, when they replied,
    Thou didst hear me.

Sev'n whole days, not one in seven,
    I will praise thee.
In my heart, though not in heaven,
    I can raise thee.

Thou grew'st soft and moist with tears,
    Thou relentedst:
And when Justice call'd for fears,
    Thou dissentedst.

Small it is, in this poor sort
    To enroll thee:
E'en eternity is too short
    To extol thee.

George Herbert

⬥⬥⬥

Come, Thou Fount of every blessing, tune my heart to sing
    Thy grace;
Streams of mercy, never ceasing, call for songs of loudest
    praise.
Teach me some melodious sonnet, sung by flaming
    tongues above;
Praise his name, I'm fixed upon it, mount of Thy
    redeeming love.

Sorrowing I shall be in spirit, till released from flesh and
    sin,
Yet from what I do inherit, here Thy praises I'll begin;
Here I raise my Ebenezer; here by Thy great help I've
    come;
And I hope, by Thy good pleasure, safely to arrive at home.

Jesus sought me when a stranger, wandering from the
    courts of God;
He, to rescue me from danger, interposed His precious
    blood;
How His kindness yet pursues me, mortal tongue can
    never tell,
Clothed in flesh, till death shall loose me, I cannot
    proclaim it well.

O to grace how great a debtor daily I'm constrained to be;
Let Thy goodness, like a fetter, bind my wandering heart
    to Thee.
Prone to wander, Lord, I feel it, prone to leave the God I
    love;
Here's my heart, O take and seal it, seal it for Thy courts
    above.

O that day when freed from sinning, I shall see Thy lovely
    face;
Clothed then in blood-washed linen, how I'll sing Thy
    sovereign grace;
Come, my Lord, no longer tarry, take my ransomed soul
    away;
Send Thine angels now to carry me to realms of endless
    day.

                                    Robert Robinson

Jesus the Christ,
you refused to turn stones into bread.
Save us from using our power,
however little,
to satisfy the demands of selfishness
in the face of the greater needs of others.
Jesus the Christ,
you refused to leap from the temple top.
Save us from displaying our skills,
however modest,
to win instant popularity
in the face of nobler calls on our abilities.
Jesus the Christ,
you refused to bend the knee to a false god.
Save us from offering our devotion,
however weak,
to cheap or easy religion
in the face of the harder path
on which you bid us to follow you.
Jesus the Christ,
give us wisdom to discern evil,
and in the face of all that is deceptively attractive
help us to choose the will of God.

The Book of Common Order

Forgive me, divine Love, for speaking only of my short-
comings and not having yet understood what it means to
let your will be done, not having allowed myself to be
poured into that mould. I have been through all your gal-
leries and admired all your paintings, but I have not yet
surrendered myself sufficiently to be worthy to receive the
strokes of your brush. Now I have at last found you, beloved Master, my Healer, my Lord, blessed Love! I will be
your disciple and learn only from you. I return like a
prodigal son, starving for your bread. I will cease to traffic
in ideas and works of piety, using them only in obedience
to you in this as in all things, and not for my own satisfac-
tion. I will devote myself exclusively to the duty of the
present moment to love you, to fulfil my obligations and
to let your will be done.

Jean Pierre de Caussade

Address to the Lord

Master of beauty, craftsman of the snowflake,
Inimitable contriver,
Endower of Earth so gorgeous & different from the boring
    Moon,
Thank you for such as it is my gift.

I have made up a morning prayer to you
containing with precision everything that most matters.

'According to Thy will' the thing begins.
It took me off & on two days. It does not aim at eloquence.

You have come to my rescue again & again
in my impassable, sometimes despairing years.
You have allowed my brilliant friends to destroy
    themselves
and I am still here, severely damaged, but functioning.

Unknowable, as I am unknown to my guinea pigs:
How can I 'love' you?
I only as far as gratitude & awe
confidently and absolutely go.

I have no idea whether we live again.
It doesn't seem likely
from either the scientific or the philosophical point of
    view
but certainly all things are possible to you,
and I believe as fixedly in the Resurrection-appearances to
    Peter
and
        to Paul
    as I believe I sit in this blue chair.
Only that may have been a special case
to establish their initiatory faith.

Whatever your end may be, accept my amazement.
May I stand until death forever at attention
for any your least instruction or enlightenment.
I even feel sure you will assist me again, Master of insight
    & beauty.
                                        John Berryman

God give me work
Till my life shall end
And life
Till my work is done.

Winifred Holtby

In your long archways poets met
and there exchanged the gems they found,
becoming mighty kings of sounds,
mild, deep, and masterful.

You are the gentle evening hour
which makes all poets similar;
you squeeze yourself into their mouths,
and, feeling proud of what they found,
they decorate your brow.

Like wings a hundred thousand harps
raise, out of silence, high your name.
And bygone breezes added to
all objects and necessities
the breath of your acclaim.

Rainer Maria Rilke

Forth in Thy Name, O Lord, I go,
My daily labor to pursue,
Thee, only Thee, resolved to know
In all I think, or speak, or do.

The task Thy wisdom hath assigned
O let me cheerfully fulfill;
In all my works Thy presence find,
And prove Thy good and perfect will.

Preserve me from my calling's snare,
And hide my simple heart above,
Above the thorns of choking care,
The gilded baits of worldly love.

Thee may I set at my right hand,
Whose eyes mine inmost substance see,
And labor on at Thy command
And offer all my works to Thee.

Give me to bear Thy easy yoke,
And every moment watch and pray,
And still to things eternal look,
And hasten to Thy glorious day.

For Thee delightfully employ
Whate'er Thy bounteous grace hath given;
And run my course with even joy,
And closely walk with Thee to Heav'n.

Charles Wesley

THE WRITER OFFERS THE WORK TO GOD

Thou, O Father, who gavest the visible light as the first-
born of thy creatures, and didst pour into man the intellectual light as the top and consummation of thy workmanship, be pleased to protect and govern this work,
which, coming from thy goodness, returneth to thy glory.
Thou, after thou hadst reviewed the works which thy
hands had made, beheldest that every thing was very good,
and thou didst rest with complacency in them. But man,
reflecting on the works which he had made, saw that all
was vanity and vexation of spirit, and could by no means
acquiesce in them. Wherefore, if we labour in thy works
with the sweat of our brows, thou wilt make us partakers
of thy vision and thy sabbath. We humbly beg that this
mind may be steadfastly in us; and that thou, by your
hands, and also by the hands of others, on whom thou
shalt bestow the same spirit, wilt please to convey a lar-
gesse of new alms to thy family of mankind. These things
we commend to thy everlasting love, by our Jesus, thy
Christ, God with us.

Francis Bacon

Lord, speak to me that I may speak
In living echoes of Thy tone;
As Thou hast sought, so let me seek
Thine erring children lost and lone.

O teach me, Lord, that I may teach
The precious things Thou dost impart;
And wing my words, that they may reach
The hidden depths of many a heart.

O give Thine own sweet rest to me,
That I may speak with soothing power
A word in season, as from Thee,
To weary ones in needful hour.

Frances R. Havergal

The Scribe's Prayer

When from my fumbling hand the tired pen falls,
And in the twilight weary droops my head;
While to my quiet heart a still voice calls,
Calls me to join my kindred of the Dead:
Grant that I may, O Lord, ere rest be mine,
Write to Thy praise one radiant, ringing line.

For all of worth that in this clay abides,
The leaping rapture and the ardent flame,
The hope, the high resolve, the faith that guides:
All, all is Thine, and liveth in Thy name:
Lord, have I dallied with the sacred fire!
Lord, have I trailed Thy glory in the mire!

E'en as a toper from the dram-shop reeling,
Sees in his garret's blackness, dazzling fair,
All that he might have been, and, heart-sick, kneeling,

Sobs in the passion of a vast despair:
So my ideal self haunts me alway —
When the accounting comes, how shall I pay?

For in the dark I grope, nor understand;
And in my heart fight selfishness and sin:
Yet, Lord, I do not seek Thy helping hand;
Rather let me my own salvation win:
Let me through strife and penitential pain
Onward and upward to the heights attain.

Yea, let me live my life, its meaning seek;
Bear myself fitly in the ringing fight;
Strive to be strong that I may aid the weak;
Dare to be true — O God! the Light, the Light!
Cometh the Dark so soon. I've mocked Thy Word;
Yet do I know Thy Love: have mercy, Lord. . . .

Robert William Service

Dear Lord, the pages are finished. At least, I think they're
finished. And now it's time to send them out into the
world — my words into your world. Let me, Lord, release
them, and let me, oh let me not want anything out of
them but what good you will do with them. Let me not
worry about "reception," which is an arrogant worry, and
not truly a worry at all, but mere desire. Let me not worry
about "success," for broken as I am, that, too, is only arro-
gance. Lord, let the words serve. If these pages are to have

a life outside of this manila folder, let them speak well to those whom you mean to hear. Then, Lord, I will know that what you gave me to work with, I have worked with; and what you gave me to use, I have used. Everything after that is up to you; so let me leave it in your hands.

And Lord, one thing more: Tomorrow, of your goodness, give me another blank page, and in your mercy, set me to it.

Gary Schmidt

His Prayer for Absolution

For those my unbaptized rhymes,
Writ in my wild unhallowed times;
For every sentence, clause and word,
That's not inlaid with thee (my Lord),
Forgive me, God, and blot each line
Out of my book, that is not thine.
But if, 'mongst all, thou find'st here one
Worthy thy benediction;
That one of all the rest, shall be
The glory of my work, and me.

Robert Herrick

Lord of galaxy and space
whose incarnate story embraced
astronomers, motherhood, poverty and glory;
weave your love within our hearts
that all our fitful stops and starts
may as myrrh
and frankincense, ascend
as prayer,
that even our short stories might unfold,
facets of love, as lustrous still
as Magi's gold.

Frank Topping

Like David in the dust, like Jesus on his knees, I humble
    myself before you, Maker of heaven and earth.
When I write, it always is for some unseen, imaginary
    audience. They stand waiting on the other side of the
    blank page, or somewhere in the deep recesses
    beyond the computer screen.
When I talk to you, it is not to such an audience — these
    imagined readers of my words. But when are my
    words ever enough for you? They dip into innocuous
    void, a bubble of inconsistent thoughts. I wonder if
    you listen on the other side.
I feel I pray words to a conception of you, which somehow

THE WRITER OFFERS THE WORK TO GOD

is a shadow of you but not you. As always, I find myself wanting the one right word. It doesn't come. I fumble along the corridors of language, and find them full of shadows and half-truths.

Strip my mind and soul naked in prayer; my fumbling words translate into your great understanding, for the One I address in the work of prayer stands as the only One who knows himself fully. Grant this miracle by your grace. Then, Lord, take the meaning of the words that you find me praying as those of praise, as need, as love.

John Timmerman

AMEN

The Writers' Biographies

A young Benjamin Franklin, who at age twenty-two already showed a facility for words and a passion for finding just the right one to express his beliefs and opinions, wrote an epitaph for himself that any writer might welcome on his gravestone:

"The Body of B. Franklin Printer; like the Cover of an old Book, Its Contents torn out, And stript of its Lettering and Gilding, Lies here, Food for Worms. But the Work shall not be wholly lost: for it will, as he believ'd, appear once more, in a new & more perfect Edition, Corrected and Amended By the Author."

Henry Alford (1810–1871) Dean of Canterbury Cathedral; editor of the works of John Donne as well as a Greek New Testament; writer of such hymns as "Come, Ye Thankful People, Come."

Dante Alighieri (c. 1265–1321) Italian poet, author of *The Divine Comedy* (1307–1321) and of the courtly *La Vita Nuova* (1295).

St. Ambrose (337?-397) Bishop of Milan, counted as one of the four doctors of the Church, author of theological and exegetical works such as *De Fide, De Spiritu Sancto,* and *De Incarnationis Dominicae Sacramento.*

Lancelot Andrewes (1555–1626) Dean of Westminster and chaplain to Queen Elizabeth; Andrewes worked as a general editor of the King James Bible; his sermons were published three years after his death.

St. Anselm (c. 1033–1109) A Benedictine monk and archbishop of Canterbury from 1093 until his death; author of *De Veritate,* asserting God as absolute Truth.

Thomas Aquinas (c. 1225–1274) Dominican monk and author of the *Summa Theologica,* considered the Church's greatest theologian and philosopher.

Thomas Arnold (1795–1842) Headmaster of Rugby School and author of sermons as well as an unfinished *History of Rome* (1838–1842).

St. Augustine (354-430) Bishop of Hippo, towering theologian and author of *Confessions* (397-398) and *City of God* (426); the patron saint of sore eyes.

Jane Austen (1775–1817) Author of six novels, including *Pride and Prejudice* (1813), *Emma* (1816), and *Mansfield Park* (1814).

Margaret Avison (1918–2007) Canadian poet whose collections include *The Dumbfounding* (1966) and *Momentary Dark* (2006); her *Selected Poems* were collected in 1991, and

Listening: The Last Poems of Margaret Avison, published two years after her death (2009).

Francis Bacon (1561–1626) Essayist and philosopher, whose *Essays* (1557) remains his best-known work.

William Barclay (1907–1978) Church of Scotland minister, author of a set of seventeen volumes of commentary on the New Testament, as well as books such as *The Plain Man Looks at the Beatitudes* (1963) and *The Plain Man Looks at the Lord's Prayer* (1964).

Richard Baxter (1615–1691) Chaplain to Charles II, author of *The Saint's Everlasting Rest* (1650) and *The Holy Common-wealth* (1659).

The Venerable Bede (c. 672-735) Priest at Wearmouth and Jarrow, scientist and historian, and author of many treatises on phenomena as diverse as the tides and music; writer of *The Ecclesiastical History of the English Church.*

Henry Ward Beecher (1813–1887) Minister of Plymouth Congregational Church in Brooklyn, brother of Harriet Beecher Stowe, editor of several religious journals and author of *Life of Jesus* (1871) and *Norwood, or Village Life in New England* (1868), a novel.

Bernard of Clairvaux (1090–1153) Cistercian abbot, author of *On the Conversion of Clerics* (1122), aimed at young priests in France, and *De Gratia et Libero Arbitrio,* on the relationship of grace and free will; writer of the text for "O Sacred Head, Now Wounded," and patron saint of beekeepers and candle makers.

Bernard of Cluny (First half of twelfth century) Writer of *De Contemptu Mundi,* satirizing the moral decay of the century, including attacks on the hierarchy of the Church, and possibly an influence on Dante's visions of heaven and hell.

John Berryman (1914–1972) American poet, one of the founders of the Confessional School of poetry, author of *The Dispossessed* (1948), *Berryman's Sonnets* (1967), and *The Dream Songs* (1969).

William Bright (1824–1901) Anglican priest and historian, educated at Rugby and University College, Oxford; editor of *Ancient Collects and Other Prayers* (1857), *Hymns and Other Poems* (1866), and *Some Aspects of Primitive Church Life* (1898).

Anne Brontë (1820–1849) The youngest of the three Bronte sisters, author of *Agnes Grey* (1847) and *The Tenant of Wildfell Hall* (1848).

Emily Brontë (1818–1848) Author of *Wuthering Heights* (1847) and, together with her sisters Charlotte and Anne, *Poems by Currier, Ellis, and Acton Bell* (1846).

Dom Helder Camara (1909–1999) Catholic archbishop in northeast Brazil, whose peace advocacy led to his *Spiral of Violence* (1971), written during the Vietnam War.

Catherine Cameron (b. 1927) Born in New Brunswick; sociologist at University of Laverne, California, author of hymns and contributor to *Contemporary Worship 1* (Inter-Lutheran Commission on Worship, 1969).

Thomas Campion (1567–1619) A musician and poet whose *Observations on the Arte of Poesie* (1602) argued for the abandonment of rhyme.

Thomas John Carlisle (1913–1992) Pastor of Stone Street Presbyterian Church in Watertown, New York, and prolific poet; author of *I Need a Century* (1963), *Journey with Job* (1976), and *Looking for Jesus: Poems in Search of the Christ of the Gospels* (1993).

Gilbert Keith Chesterton (1874–1936) Artist, poet, novelist, critic and essayist, a prolific publisher (over 100 titles) and a distinctive stylist. In 1922 he was received into the Catholic Church by Father O'Connor, the model for his popular detective, Father Brown.

Michael John Radford Counsell (b. 1935) Author of plays and the first Creole translations of the Gospels; compiler of *Prayers for Sundays* (1994) and *2000 Years of Prayer* (1999).

Fanny Crosby (1820–1915) Prolific hymn writer of over eight thousand hymns, among them "Blessed Assurance," "All the Way My Savior Leads Me," "Draw Me Nearer," and "To God Be the Glory"; poet whose collections include *A Blind Girl and Other Poems* (1844) and *A Wreath of Columbia's Flowers* (1858).

Chris Crowe (b. 1954) Author of middle grade and young adult works that explore African American history, including *Mississippi, 1955* (2002), *Getting Away with Murder* (2003), and *Thurgood Marshall (Up Close)* (2008).

e. e. cummings (1894–1962) Poet, critic, and dramatist. His more than fifteen books of poetry are known for their unusual typography, punctuation, and syntax. *The Complete Poems 1913–1962* was first published in 1972.

Jean Pierre de Caussade (1675–1751) French Jesuit priest, author of *On Prayer* (1741) and the still-popular *Abandonment to Divine Providence*.

Charles de Foucauld (1858–1916) Martyred priest who ministered in Algeria; his work led to the founding of the Little Brothers of Jesus after his death.

John Donne (1572–1631) Poet and Dean of St. Paul's, he showed himself among the greatest of the metaphysical poets with works such as *An Anatomy of the World* (1611) and *Divine Poems* (1633).

John Dryden (1631–1700) Restoration poet, dramatist, and critic, known for his *Don Sebastian* (1690); *King Arthur* (1691), and his last play, *Love Triumphant* (1694) — and most particularly for his "Essay on Dramatick Poesie" (1668).

Colin Duriez (b. 1947) Writer on the work of the Inklings; author of *The C. S. Lewis Handbook* (1990), *The Inklings Handbook* (2001), and *Tolkien and The Lord of the Rings* (2001).

Marian Wright Edelman (b. 1939) Winner of a MacArthur Prize Fellowship, and author of *The Measure of Our Success: A Letter to My Children and Yours.*

T. S. Eliot (1888–1965) Literary critic, dramatist, poet, whose *Prufrock and Other Observations* (1917) and, more especially, *The Wasteland* (1922), established him as a poet, and whose *Murder in the Cathedral* (1935) and *The Cocktail Party* (1949) established him as a dramatist.

Christopher Ellis (b. 1951) Former principal of Bristol Baptist College and currently pastor of West Bridgford Baptist Church; editor of *Gathering for Worship: Patterns of Prayers for the Community of Disciples* (2005) and author of *Approaching God* (2009).

Susan Felch (b. 1951) Editor of *The Collected Works of Anne*

Vaughan Lock (1999); *Elizabeth Tyrwhit's Morning and Evening Prayers* (2008); and *Elizabeth I and Her Age* (2009).

Benjamin Franklin (1706–1790) American printer, inventor, scientist, diplomat, and writer, whose *Autobiography,* published after his death, helped to establish American letters.

Johann Freylinghausen (1670–1736) Lutheran pastor of the St. Ulrich Church in Halle, composer of forty-four hymns, including "Jesus, Thou Source of Calm Repose."

Beth Fritsch American religious poet, author of "Love Made Visible" and "O Impermanence," collected in Macrina Wiederkehr's *Seven Sacred Pauses* (2008).

Robert Frost (1874–1963) After *A Boy's Will* (1913) and *North of Boston* (1914), he became professor of poetry at Harvard University and published works such as *New Hampshire* (1923), *West-Running Brook* (1928), and *Steeple Bush* (1947).

Thomas Fuller (1608–1661) Chaplain to Charles II, theologian and historian, author of such works as *The Holy State and the Profane State* (1642) and *Worthies of England* (1662).

Douglas Galbraith Musician, theologian, hymn writer, and member of the Iona Community, he co-edited *Common Ground* (1998), an ecumenical anthology of hymns for Scottish churches.

Margaret Gibson (b. 1944) Professor Emerita of the University of Connecticut, author of collections of poetry such as *The Vigil* (1993) and *Icon and Evidence* (2001), as well as a prose memoir, *The Prodigal Daughter: Reclaiming an Unfinished Childhood* (2008).

Jacob Glatshteyn (1896–1971) Polish-born American poet

who powerfully influenced Yiddish literature in works such as *A Jew from Lublin* (1966).

Louise Glück (b. 1943) American poet, author of *The Wild Iris* (1992) — which won the Pulitzer Prize — as well as *Vita Nova* (1999), *Averno* (2006), and *A Village Life: Poems* (2009).

Mary Gordon (b. 1949) Catholic novelist and memoirist; author of *Circling My Mother: A Memoir* (2007); and novels *Men and Angels* (1985), *Spending* (1998), and *Pearl* (2005); her stories were collected in 2006.

Nikki Grimes (b. 1950) American poet, picture book author, and middle grade and young adult novelist, author of such books as *A Girl Named Mister* (2010), *The Road to Paris* (2006), *My Man Blue* (2002), and *Meet Danitra Brown* (1997).

Donald Hall (b. 1928) Writer of more than fifteen books of poetry, author of children's books, memoirs, and literary criticism; long-time teacher of the University of Michigan, before he left to return to his ancestral home in New Hampshire, where he became Poet Laureate of the United States.

Dag Hammarskjöld (1905–1961) Secretary-General of the United Nations, whose journal was published after his death as *Markings* (1963).

Frances Ridley Havergal (1836–1879) Author of such hymns as "Take My Life and Let It Be" and "Like a River Glorious," as well as posthumously published works such as *Little Pillows, or Goodnight Thoughts for the Little Ones* (1880).

Robert Hayden (1913–1980) American poet, who in works like *Heart-Shape in the Dust* (1940), *Words in the Mourning Time* (1970), and *Angle of Ascent* (1975) lyrically evoked the sufferings and achievements of African Americans; appointed Consultant in Poetry to the Library of Congress, 1976.

David Head (b. 1922) Author of studies and collections of prayers such as *He Sent Leanness* (1959), *Stammerer's Tongue* (1960), and *Shout for Joy* (1962).

George Herbert (1593–1633) Religious poet, essayist, Anglican divine, author of *The Temple* (1633) and *A Priest to the Temple, or The Country Parson* (1652).

Robert Herrick (1591–1674) Sometimes described as "frankly pagan," Herrick's poetry was published in *Noble Numbers or Pious Pieces* (1647) and, more famously, in his *Hesperides, or Works Both Human and Divine* (1648).

Donald R. Hettinga (1953) Author of literary criticism such as *Presenting Madeleine L'Engle* (1993) and a biography for young readers: *The Brothers Grimm: Two Lives, One Legacy* (2001).

Hilary of Poitiers (315-368) Orator who converted to Christianity at age 35; his most important book is his twelve-volume *On the Trinity;* the first Latin hymn writer of the Church.

Scott Hoezee (b. 1964) American minister, author of such theological works as *The Riddle of Grace* (1996), *Remember Creation* (1998), and *Proclaim the Wonder: Preaching Science on Sunday* (2003).

Winifred Holtby (1898–1935) British writer and pacifist, author of novels such as *Anderby Wold* (1923), *The Land of Green Ginger* (1927), and *South Riding* (1936), and the writer of a critical study of Virginia Woolf.

Nancy Hull (b. 1952) Sports writer and children's book reviewer; author of the young adult novel, *On Rough Seas* (2008).

Helen Hunt Jackson (1830–1885) Massachusetts novelist whose *A Century of Dishonor* (1881) and *Ramona* (1884) both fought vigorously for the rights of Native Americans.

Samuel Johnson (1709–1784) This great lexicographer, critic, and poet is today best known for his *Dictionary of the English Language* (1755), though he also published an edition of Shakespeare (1765) and *Lives of the Poets* (1779–81).

Thomas Ken (1637–1711) Hymnist, author of *Morning, Evening, and Midnight Hymns* as well as a manual of prayers.

Johannes Kepler (1571–1630) German mathematician and astronomer whose devout Lutheranism heavily influenced his scientific writings.

Søren Aaby Kierkegaard (1813–1855) Danish theologian and philosopher, who argued that action in faith and love requires a leap beyond evidence in books such as *Philosophical Fragments* (1844), *Works of Love* (1847), *Christian Discourses* (1848), and *Practice in Christianity* (1850).

Edward King (1829–1910) Bishop of Lincoln and author of *Spiritual Letters* (1910).

Charles Kingsley (1819–1875) Theologian and novelist, author of *Westward Ho!* (1855) and, his most enduring work, *The Water Babies* (1863). Ten years after its publication he became Canon of Westminster.

L. S. Klatt (b. 1962) American poet, author of *Interloper* (2009) and *Cloud of Ink* (2011).

Madeleine L'Engle (1918–2007) Young adult writer known best for her Time Quartet: *A Wrinkle in Time* (1962), *A Wind* in the Door (1973), *A Swiftly Tilting Planet* (1978), and *Many Waters* (1986), as well as her Crosswicks journals (1972–1988).

Denise Levertov (1923–1997) British-born American poet, author of *The Poet in the World* (1973); and the collections *The Life Around Us: Selected Poems on Nature* (1997), *The Stream and the Sapphire* (1997), and *This Great Unknowing: Last Poems* (2000).

C. S. Lewis (1898–1963) Novelist, theologian, and critic, author of *The Allegory of Love* (1936), *The Screwtape Letters* (1942), *Mere Christianity* (1952), as well as the Narnia Chronicles, beginning with *The Lion, the Witch and the Wardrobe* (1950).

George MacDonald (1824–1905) Theologian and novelist, author of romances such as *The Marquis of Lossie* (1877) and children's novels such as *At the Back of the North Wind* (1871).

Katherine Mansfield (1888–1923) Writer of short fiction in the early Modernist tradition, and author of such well-known stories as "The Garden Party" and "The Fly."

Peter Marshall (1902–1949) Pastor of Westminster Presbyterian Church in Atlanta and twice the chaplain of the United States Senate, his sermons and prayers were published by his wife Catherine Marshall, who also wrote his biography: *A Man Called Peter* (1951).

John Masefield (1878–1967) Poet Laureate, author of the war adventures *Gallipoli* (1916) and *The Old Forest Line* (1917), as well as work brought together in his *Collected Poems* (1923).

John Mason (1645–1694) Rector of Water Stratford in Buckinghamshire, one of the earliest writers of hymns in the Church of England.

Susan McCaslin (b. 1947) Canadian poet and scholar, author of fourteen collections of poetry, including *At the Mercy Seat* (2003), *Lifting the Stone* (2007), and *Demeter Goes Skydiving* (2011).

Thomas Merton (1915–1968) Trappist monk, poet, and author of over 70 books on issues of literature and faith, including the autobiographical *The Seven-Storey Mountain* (1948).

W. S. Merwin (b. 1927) American poet, winner of two Pulitzer Prizes (1971 and 2009), author of *The Moving Target* (1963), *The Compass Flower* (1977), *The Shadow of Sirius* (2008).

Edna St. Vincent Millay (1892–1950) Lyric poet and dramatist. She was awarded the Pulitzer Prize for *The Harp-Weaver* (1923) and became one of the most popular poets of her day with volumes like *The Buck in the Snow* (1928), *Huntsman, What Quarry?* (1939) and *Make Bright the Arrows* (1942).

Vassar Miller (1924–1998) American poet who triumphed over her cerebral palsy to write such works as *Adam's Footprint* (1956) and *Wage War on Silence* (1961), nominated for a Pulitzer Prize; her poems were collected in 1991.

John Milton (1608–1674) Poet of *Paradise Lost* (1667), followed by *Samson Agonistes* (1671), written during his blindness.

William R. Mitchell (b. 1930) American poet, professor emeritus of English at Oklahoma Baptist University, author of *Tribute to the Advent* (1990) and the autobiographical *My Life Before the Fire* (2007).

James Montgomery (1771–1854) Poet and hymn writer, the most famous of which is "For Ever with the Lord."

Dwight Lyman Moody (1837–1899) American preacher,

whose popularity brought thousands to hear him speak on his evangelism campaigns throughout the United States and Great Britain; author of collections of his sermons.

Sir Thomas More (1478-1535) The Lord Chancellor murdered by Henry VIII; historian, and author of *Utopia* (1515-1516).

John Henry Newman (1801-1890) Anglican curate whose conversion to Catholicism he described in his *Apologia pro Vita Sua* (1864); known for his *Idea of a University* (1852).

Reinhold Niebuhr (1892-1971) American theologian, who set Christianity in the arena of American politics in books such as *The Nature and Destiny of Man* (1941), *Moral Man and Immoral Society* (1932), and *The Irony of American History* (1952).

Henri Nouwen (1932-1996) Catholic theologian, author of *Road to Daybreak* (1990), *Return of the Prodigal Son: A Meditation on Fathers, Brothers, and Sons* (1992), and minister at the L'Arche community in Toronto.

Hughes Oliphant Old (b. 1933) Professor of Reformed Theology and Worship at Erskine Theological Seminary; author of *Leading in Prayer: A Workbook for Ministers* (1995) and *Worship* (1984, 2002).

Alan Paton (1903-1988) South African writer and activist against apartheid; author of *Cry, the Beloved Country* (1948).

Jessica Powers (1905-1988) An American poet and Carmelite nun, author of *The Lantern Burns* (1939), *Journey to Bethlehem* (1980), and *The House at Rest* (1984). Her *Selected Poetry* was published in 1989.

Michael Quoist (1921-1997) French priest and writer, author of the hugely popular *Prayers of Life* (1954), and works such as *Christ Is Alive* (1971) and *Meet Christ and Live* (1973).

Walter Rauschenbusch (1861–1918) Known as the "father of the Social Gospel," he authored *Christianity and the Social Crisis* (1907) and *Christianizing the Social Order* (1912).

Debra Rienstra (b. 1965) Poet and theological writer, author of *Great with Child: Reflections on Faith, Fullness, and Becoming a Mother* (2002) and *So Much More: An Invitation to Christian Spirituality* (2005).

Rainer Maria Rilke (1875–1926) Austrian poet and critic of the arts, his most famous prose work is *Letters to a Young Poet,* first translated into English in 1934; his most popular poetic work is *Duino Elegies* (1922).

Robert Robinson (1735–1790) British Methodist minister, composer of "Come, Thou Fount of Every Blessing."

Christina Rossetti (1830–1894) Pre-Raphaelite poet, author of *Goblin Market and Other Poems* (1862), *A Pageant and Other Poems* (1881), and a collection of children's poetry, *Sing-Song* (1872).

Gary D. Schmidt (b. 1957) Writer of middle grade and young adult novels such as *The Wednesday Wars* (2007); co-editor of the present volume.

Otto Selles (b. 1964) American poet, author of *New Songs: A Collection* (2001).

Joe Seremane (b. 1938) South African political leader and frequently jailed activist against apartheid; the founding chair of the multi-racial Democratic Alliance party.

Robert William Service (1874–1958) Canadian writer, whose service in World War I led to *Rhymes of a Red Cross Man*

(1916); he also published frontier poems as in *Ballads of a Cheechako* (1909) and novels such as *The Roughneck* (1923).

Luci Shaw (b. 1928) Poet, non-fiction writer, editor, author of, most recently, *Harvesting Fog* (2010).

Christopher Smart (1722–1771) Poet — a contemporary and friend of Samuel Johnson — who produced his greatest work, *Song to David* (1763) while under confinement for madness.

Aleksandr Solzhenitsyn (1918–2008) Russian historian and novelist, whose work — such as *One Day in the Life of Ivan Denisovich* (1962) — led to a Nobel Prize in 1970, but whose criticism of Soviet Russia — such as *The Gulag Archipelago* (1973–1978) — led to a twenty-year exile.

Robert Louis Stevenson (1850–1894) British poet, novelist, and essayist, whose range varied from adventure books such as *Treasure Island* (1883) and *The Black Arrow* (1888) to *A Child's Garden of Verses* (1885).

Elizabeth Stickney (b. 1958) Author of *The Loving Arms of God* (2001), illustrated by Helen Cann; co-editor of the present volume.

Edward Taylor (1642–1729) Poet and divine in colonial Massachusetts, author of *Preparatory Meditations* (1682–1725) and *God's Determinations Touching His Elect* (c. 1680); his complete poems were not published until 1960.

Alfred, Lord Tennyson (1809–1892) Victorian poet who assumed the role of Poet Laureate upon the death of Wordsworth, and author of poems that spoke the temper of his times: "Ulysses," "The Lotus Eaters," "The Lady of Shalott," "The Charge of the Light Brigade."

R. S. Thomas (1913–2000) Fierce Welsh nationalist, poet, and Anglican clergyman, known especially for his *Song at the Year's Turning* (1955) and *Laboratories of the Spirit* (1978).

John Timmerman (b. 1945) Novelist, devotional writer, and literary critic; author of *Jane Kenyon: A Literary Life* (2002) and *A Season of Suffering* (1987).

Frank Topping (b. 1937) Ordained a Methodist minister in 1970, and Warden of John Wesley's Chapel, Bristol; author, playwright, and editor of books such as *Daily Prayer* (2003).

Sandy Tritt (b. 1957) Novelist and president of the Ohio Valley Literary Group, author of *Living the Legacy* (1998), CEO of Inspiration for Writers, Inc. (www.InspirationForWriters .com).

William J. Vande Kopple (b. 1949) Linguist and author of studies such as *Clear and Coherent Prose* (1989) and collections of creative essays such as *The Catch: Families, Fishing, and Faith* (2004) and *The Release* (2009).

James Vanden Bosch (b. 1948) Linguist and columnist, author of *Ask Anonymous: A Collection* (2005).

Elizabeth Vander Lei (b. 1963) Rhetorician and linguist, editor with Bonnie Lenore Kyburz of *Negotiating Religious Faith in the Composition Classroom* (2005) and author with Dean Ward of *Real Texts: Reading and Writing Across the Disciplines* (2008; 2012).

Walter Wangerin, Jr. (b. 1944) Lutheran minister, Jochum Chair at Valparaiso University, author of works such as *The Book of the Dun Cow* (1978), *Ragman and Other Cries of Faith* (1996), *The Book of God* (1996), and *Naomi and Her Daughters* (2010).

Isaac Watts (1674–1748) Writer of over 500 hymns, author of *Horae Lyricae* (1706), *Hymns* (1707), and *Metrical Psalms* (1719), as well as a *Guide to Prayer* (1715).

Charles Wesley (1707–1788) Methodist minister and writer of hymns such as "Jesus, Lover of My Soul" and "Hark! the Herald Angels Sing."

Susanna Wesley (1669–1749) Mother of Charles Wesley, and known as the Mother of Methodism; she wrote meditations and commentaries upon scriptural passages as part of her children's spiritual educations.

John Greenleaf Whittier (1807–1892) Quaker poet, whose many collections include *Songs of Labor* (1850), *The Panorama* (1856), *In War Time* (1864), and his most popular work, *Snow-Bound* (1866).

Macrina Wiederkehr Benedictine monastic of St. Scholastic Monastery in Fort Smith, Arkansas, author of books on prayer such as *The Song of the Seed* (1995) and *Seven Sacred Pauses* (2008).

Paul Willis (b. 1955) Novelist, poet, and essayist, author of *Bright Shoots of Everlastingness: Essays on Faith and the American Wild* (2005) and *Rising from the Dead* (2009).

Sources and Acknowledgments

Working on a project such as this teaches us about the goodness of others. So here we name James Bratt, and Cindy deJong, and Debra Freeburg, and Susan Felch, and Jenny Williams, and thank them for suggesting and providing and tracking down selections for this anthology. Our work would have been more daunting, the result less pleasing without their help.

Alford: From Henry Alford, *The Year of Prayer, Being Family Prayers for the Christian Year* (London: Alexander Strahan, 1867): 28, 47.

Ambrose: Prayer attributed to Ambrose, translated by John Henry Newman and John Mason Neale, and included as the hymn for None in the *Short Breviary*.

Andrewes: "Thou who sendest forth," from *Preces Privatae*, printed as *Lancelot Andrewes and his Private Devotions* (Edinburgh: T. and A. Constable, 1896; first published Oxford, 1675).

St. Anselm: "Holy and undivided Trinity," from the first prayer in Anselm's *Meditations and Prayers*. "My whole heart, speak now," from the opening chapter of Anselm's *The Proslogion* (written 1077–1078).

Aquinas: "O Infinite Creator," from Oratio S. Thomae Aquinatis ante stadium, "The Prayer of St. Thomas Before Study."

Arnold: "I have work to do" is the prayer Arnold used as he entered Rugby School each day; it is recorded in his sermon, "How to Nourish the Spirit of Prayer," included in his *Christian Life, Its Course, Its Hindrances, and Its Helps: Sermons, Preached Mostly in the Chapel of Rugby School* (London: B. Fellowes, 1841): 84. "O Lord, who by Thy holy Apostle," from *The Life and Correspondence of Thomas Arnold, D.D.*, ed. Arthur Penrhyn Stanley (London: B. Fellowes, 1845): 2: 347.

St. Augustine: From *Confessions* 1.1, here translated by William Watts in 1631, with emendations by the editors.

Austen: "Give us grace" is one of three prayers by Austen first collected in 1926 and published in *The Works of Jane Austen*, ed. R. W. Chapman (Oxford: Oxford University Press, 1954; 1988): 6: 453. By permission of Oxford University Press.

Avison: From *Always Now: Collected Poems* (Erin, Ontario: The Porcupine's Quill, 2003): 192. Used by permission of The Porcupine's Quill and the Estate of Margaret Avison.

Bacon: "To God the Father" (The Student's Prayer); "Thou, O Father" (The Writer's Prayer); and "O Eternal God" are from Bacon's *Christian Paradoxes,* and published in *The Works of Francis Bacon,* ed. James Spedding (London: Longmans, 1852): 7: 259-261.

Barclay: "Let thy Spirit," from *A Book of Everyday Prayers* (New York: Harper and Brothers, 1959). "Be on our lips" and "Eternal God," from *A Plain Man's Book of Prayers* (London: Collins, 1928): 38 and 52. "Thank you, O God," from *More Prayers for the Plain Man* (London: Collins, 1962).

Baxter: "My Lord, I have nothing to do in this world," from "Dying Thoughts on Philippians 1.23," recorded in *The Practical Works of the Rev. Richard Baxter,* William Orme, ed. (London: James

Duncan, 1830): 402-403. "But O Thou, the Merciful," from *The Saint's Everlasting Rest* (London: Thomas Underhill, 1654): Part IV: 303-304.

Bede: "And now, I beseech thee," from the autobiographical conclusion to Bede's *Ecclesiastical History of the English People*. Translated here by J. A. Giles in *The Venerable Bede's Ecclesiastical History of England, also the Anglo-Saxon Chronicle* (London: Henry G. Bohn, 1849).

Beecher: From *Prayers from Plymouth Pulpit* (New York: Charles Scribner and Company, 1867). From the prayer, "Christ Our Necessity and Joy."

Belgic Confession: A sixteenth-century confession authored by Guido de Brès, a reformed minister who lived in the Netherlands. The prayer was written in 1561, and after several amendments was adopted by the Synod of Dort in 1618–1619 as a doctrinal standard. Text taken from *Psalter Hymnal* (Grand Rapids, MI: CRC Publications, 1987), with permission.

Bernard of Clairvaux: "Jesus, the very thought of Thee," trans. Edward Caswall (1814-1876) from Bernard's long poem, "Dulcis Jesu Memorial," and published in Caswall's *Lyra Catholic* (1849).

Bernard of Cluny: From the dedicatory epistle for "Hora Novissima, Tempora Pessima Sunt, Vigilemus," composed in the Abbey of Cluny in 1145.

Berryman: "Address to the Lord," Section 1 from "Eleven Addresses to the Lord," from *Collected Poems, 1937–1971* by John Berryman. Copyright © 1989 by Kate Donahue Berryman. Reprinted by permission of Farrar, Straus and Giroux, LLC.

Book of Common Order: "Jesus the Christ, you refused to turn stones into bread," a prayer from the *Book of Common Order,* Mission and Discipleship Council, Church of Scotland, 121 George Street, Edinburgh EH2 4YN. Used with the permission of the Church of Scotland.

Bright: "O Lord God, in whom we live" and "Almighty God, who hast sent," from *Ancient Collects and Other Prayers* (Oxford: J. H. and James Parker, 1857).

Brontë, Anne: "The Doubter's Prayers," from *Poems by Currier, Ellis, and Acton Bell* (London: Aylott and Jones, 1846).

Brontë, Emily: "No Coward Soul Is Mine," from *Poems by Currier, Ellis, and Acton Bell* (London: Aylott and Jones, 1846).

Camara: Taken from *A Thousand Reasons for Living*, by Dom Helder Camara, ed. José de Broucher, trans. Alan Neame, published and copyright 1981 by Darton, Longman and Todd Ltd, London, and used by permission of the publishers.

Cameron: "God, who stretched the spangled heavens" — words by Catherine Cameron. Copyright © 1967 Hope Publishing Co., Carol Stream, IL 60188. All rights reserved. Used by permission.

Campion: "To Music bent is my retired Mind," first published in Campion's *Two Bookes of Ayres* (London, 1613).

Carlisle: "Help the Blind," from his *Looking for Jesus* (Grand Rapids, MI: William B. Eerdmans, 1993): 68. Used by permission of William B. Eerdmans Publishing Co.

Chesterton: "You say grace before meals" is quoted in Dudley Barker, *G. K. Chesterton, a Biography* (New York: Stein and Day, 1973): 65, from unpublished notebook jottings. "A Hymn: O God of Earth and Altar," originally printed in *The Commonwealth*, then given to the editor of the *English Hymnal*, Percy Dearmer, who published it in 1906.

Conference of European Churches: "Lord God, we have given more weight to our successes" is from the Conference of European Churches worship book, *Gloria Deo: Worship Book for Conference of European Churches, Assembly IX, Stirling, Scotland*. Copyright © Conference of European Churches, Geneva, Switzerland. Used with permission.

Counsell: "Almighty God, dwelling in the beauty of holiness" and "God, who wrestled with chaos," from *2000 Years of Prayer*, edited by Michael Counsell (Harrisburg, PA: Morehouse Publishing, 1999): 564, 563. Copyright © 1999 by Morehouse Publishing, Harrisburg, PA. All rights reserved. Used by permission of Church Publishing Incorporated, New York, NY.

Crosby: "A Reverie," written in 1903, and first printed in Fanny

Crosby's autobiography, *Memories of Eighty Years* (Boston: James H. Earle and Company, 1906).

Crowe: Text original to this collection, with permission.

Cummings: "i thank You God for most this amazing." Copyright 1950, © 1978, 1991 by the Trustees for the E. E. Cummings Trust. Copyright © by George James Firmage, from *Complete Poems 1904–1962*, by E. E. Cummings, edited by George J. Firmage. Used by permission of Liveright Publishing Corporation.

Dante: From "Paradiso," *The Divine Comedy*, Canto 33, ll. 67-75, 101-106, when Dante is guided by Beatrice to Paradise. This text from the first English translation of Dante by Henry Wadsworth Longfellow (Boston: Ticknor and Fields, 1867).

De Caussade: "O Unknown Love" and "Forgive me, divine Love," from a collection of letters to sisters at Nancy, first published in 1861, and then more authoritatively as *L'abandon à la providence divine* (Paris: Desclée de Brouwer, 1966). Translated by Algar Labouchere Thorold in *Self-Abandonment to the Divine Providence* (London: Burns, Oates & Co., 1933). Jean Pierre de Caussade copyright 1933. Reproduced by kind permission of Continuum International Publishing Group.

De Foucauld: "O Lord, guide my thoughts and my words," from *The Spiritual Autobiography of Charles de Foucauld*, edited by Jean-François Six, translated by J. Holland Smith (New York: P. J. Kenedy, 1964; rpt. Denville, NJ: Dimension Books, 1972).

Donne: "When we see any man," from Sermon 8, preached upon Whitsunday 1626 on John 16.8, 9, 10, 11; quoted from *The Sermons of John Donne* (London: Cambridge University Press, 1954): 7: 215-236. "Keep us Lord," from Sermon 146, preached at Whitehall in 1627; quoted from *The Works of John Donne*, ed. Henry Alford (London: John W. Parker, 1839): 5: 604-623. "My God, my God," from Expostulation and Prayer 19 of *Devotions upon Emergent Occasions*, first published London: Thomas Jones, 1624.

Dryden: "Creator Spirit," translated by Dryden from "Veni, Creator Spiritus," by Rabanus Maurus, in 1690.

Duriez: "On Prayer," printed in *The Country of the Risen King: An Anthology of Christian Poetry*, ed. Merle Meeter (Grand Rapids, MI: Baker Book House, 1978): 72.

Edelman: From *Guide My Feet* by Marian Wright Edelman. © 1995 by Marian Wright Edelman. Reprinted by permission of Beacon Press, Boston.

Eliot: "The soul of Man" and "Lord, shall we not bring these gifts" from "Choruses from 'The Rock'" (IX) from *Collected Poems 1909–1962* by T. S. Eliot, copyright 1936 by Harcourt, Inc. and renewed 1964 by T. S. Eliot, reprinted by permission of Houghton Mifflin Harcourt Publishing Company.

Ellis: "Spirit of God, you are the breath of creation," from Janet Morley, ed., *Bread of Tomorrow: Prayers for the Church Year* (London: SPCK, 1992): 126. Reprinted by permission of Christian Aid.

Felch: Texts original to this collection, with permission.

Franklin: The epitaph is preserved in papers owned by Franklin's grandson, William Temple Franklin, and held by the Library of Congress.

Freylinghausen: Freylinghausen's hymns were published in his *Geistreiches Gesangbuch* (Halle, 1704/1714).

Fritsch: "Love Made Visible," from *Seven Sacred Pauses: Living Mindfully Through the Hours of the Day*, ed. Macrina Wiederkerhr (Notre Dame, IN: Sorin Books, 2008): 88-89.

Frost: From *A Boy's Will* (New York: Henry Holt and Company, 1915).

Fuller: "Gracious Lord," from *Pulpit Sparks, or Choice Forms of Prayer, by Several Reverend and Godly Divines* (London: W. Gilbertson, 1659): 156-171.

Galbraith: "Creator God," excerpt from *The Pattern of Our Days: Worship in the Celtic Tradition from the Iona Community*. Edited by Kathy Galloway. Copyright © 1996 by The Authors. Paulist Press, Inc., New York/Mahwah, NJ. Reprinted by permission of Paulist Press, Inc. www.paulistpress.com.

Gibson: "Poetry Is the Spirit of the Dead, Watching," published in

Margaret Gibson, *One Body* (Louisiana State University Press, 2007). Copyright © Margaret Gibson. Reprinted by permission of Louisiana State University Press.

Glatshteyn: "Without Offerings," from *American Yiddish Poetry,* ed. Benjamin and Barbara Harshav (Berkeley: University of California Press, 1986). Copyright © 1986. Reprinted by permission of University of California Press.

Glück: "Vespers," from *The Wild Iris* (New York: The Ecco Press, 1992). Copyright © 1992 by Louise Glück. Reprinted by permission of HarperCollins Publishers.

Gordon: "For Those Whose Work Is Invisible," from the poem series "Prayers." "Prayers" by Mary Gordon was first published in *The Paris Review* (Issue 151, Summer, 1999). Used with the permission of *The Paris Review* and reprinted by permission of SLL/Sterling Lord Literistic, Inc. Copyright by Mary Gordon.

Grimes: "Prayer and Meditation for *A Girl Named Mister,*" text original to this collection, with permission. Drafted on the occasion of writing *A Girl Named Mister* (Grand Rapids, MI: Zondervan, 2010).

Hall: "A Grace," from *Old and New Poems* by Donald Hall. Copyright © 1990 by Donald Hall. Reprinted by permission of Houghton Mifflin Harcourt Publishing Company. All rights reserved.

Hammarskjöld: From *Markings,* Dag Hammarskjöld's spiritual diary published after his death: *Markings,* translated by W. H. Auden and Leif Sjöberg, translation copyright © 1964, copyright renewed 2002 by Alfred A. Knopf, a division of Random House, Inc., and Faber and Faber Ltd. Used by permission of Alfred A. Knopf, a division of Random House, Inc.

Havergal: "Lord, Speak to Me" was written at Winterdyne, England, in 1872 for the use of lay helpers in the church of Frances Havergal; it was originally called "The Worker's Prayer."

Hayden: "Ice Storm." Copyright © 1982 by Irma Hayden, from *Collected Poems of Robert Hayden* by Robert Hayden, edited by

Frederick Glaysher. Used by permission of Liveright Publishing Corporation.

Head: "Grant, I beseech thee," from *He Sent Leanness: A book of prayers for the natural man* (New York: Macmillan, and Epworth Press, 1959): 9. "With Thy Spirit," from *Stammerer's Tongue* (New York: Macmillan, and Epworth Press, 1960): 68. "In my writing on earth," from *Shout for Joy* (New York: Macmillan, and Epworth Press, 1962): 74-75. Copyright © Trustees for Methodist Church Purposes. Used by permission.

Herbert: "Sonnet 1" is from Izaak Walton's *The Life of Mr. George Herbert* (1670). "The Elixir," "Gratefulness," and "Praise (2)" are from Herbert's collection, *The Temple* (Cambridge, 1633).

Herrick: "His Prayer for Absolution," from *Herperides* (London: John Williams and F. Eglesfield, 1648).

Hettinga: Text original to this collection, with permission.

Hilary of Poitiers: A prayer based on his sermon, "On the Trinity" (Lib. 1: 37-38).

Hoezee: Texts original to this collection, with permission.

Holtby: Text written on her gravestone, Rudstone, Yorkshire.

Hull: "This Writer's Plea," text original to this collection, with permission.

Jackson: From "A Last Prayer," from her *Sonnets and Lyrics* (Boston: Roberts Brothers, 1888).

Johnson: "Lord, my maker and protector," and "Almighty God, our heavenly Father," from Johnson's *Prayers and Meditations* (London, 1785), a work published after his death and edited by Arthur Murphy in *The Works of Samuel Johnson* (London: S. and R. Bentley, 1823): 2: 698. "O God, who hast hitherto supported me," is an entry in Johnson's diary, April 3, 1753, during his compiling of his *Dictionary of the English Language*. It is printed in James Boswell, *The Life of Samuel Johnson* (London: J. Dent, 1906): 2: 152.

Ken: "Prosper thou" from "Directions for Prayer, for the Diocese of Bath and Wells," in *The Prose Works of the Right Rev. Father in*

God, Thomas Ken, ed. James Thomas Round (London: J. G. and
F. Rivington, 1838): 351.

Kepler: From *Harmonices Mundi, Harmony of the World* (1619).

Kierkegaard: "Lord, give us weak eyes" is the epigraph Kierkegaard
used for his *Sickness unto Death (Sygdomen Til Doden* [Copenha-
gen: C. A. Reitzels Forlag, 1849]). Kierkegaard attributed the
quote to the Moravian Bishop Johann Baptist von Albertini.
"How could anything rightly be said" and "Father in heaven!
Show us a little patience" are both from *The Prayers of
Kierkegaard,* ed. Perry D. Lefevre (Chicago: University of Chicago Press, 1956): 11, 19. Used by permission of the University of
Chicago Press.

King: From his sermon, "Thanksgiving," "preached at Lincoln Cathedral at the special service of Thanksgiving after the cessation
of the typhoid epidemic in that City, June, 1905," in *Sermons
and Addresses by Edward King* (London: Longmans, Green and
Co., 1911): 30-39.

Kingsley: "Stir us up," from "The Crucifixion," in *Twenty-Five Village Sermons* (Philadelphia: H. Hooker, 1854).

Klatt: "A Poet's Prayer," text original to this collection, with permission.

L'Engle: From *Walking on Water: Reflections on Faith and Art*
(Wheaton, IL: Harold Shaw Publishers, 1980): 22.

Levertov: "Flickering Mind," from *A Door in the Hive,* copyright ©
1989 by Denise Levertov. Reprinted by permission of New Directions Publishing Corp.

Lewis: "Footnote to All Prayers" and "The Apologist's Evening
Prayer" from *POEMS* by C. S. Lewis, copyright © 1964 by the Ex-
ecutors of the Estate of C. S. Lewis and renewed 1992 by C. S.
Lewis Pte. Ltd., reprinted by permission of Houghton Mifflin
Harcourt Publishing Company.

MacDonald: "Shall the Dead Praise Thee?" from *The Poetical Works
of George MacDonald* (London: Chatto and Windus, 1893): 2: 326.

Mansfield: Cited from her journal in Isabel Constance Clarke, *Six*

Portraits (London: Hutchinson, 1935): 277. Her journal was first published in 1927.

Marshall: "Lord, teach us to pray," from Catherine Marshall, ed., *The Prayers of Peter Marshall* (New York: McGraw-Hill, 1954): 15. Used by permission of Chosen, a division of Baker Publishing Company, copyright © 1989.

Masefield: "O Christ who holds," from "The Everlasting Mercy" (London: Sidgwick & Jackson, 1911); also printed in *The Oxford Book of English Mystical Verse,* ed. D. H. S. Nicholson and A. H. E. Lee (Oxford: Clarendon Press, 1917).

Mason: "How shall I sing that majesty," from his *Spiritual Songs, or Songs of Praise* (London: 1683).

McCaslin: "Master," from her chapbook *Pleroma* (copyright © 1976). Used with permission of the author.

Merton: "A Prayer to God the Father on the Vigil of Pentecost," from *Conjectures of a Guilty Bystander* by Thomas Merton, copyright © 1965, 1966 by The Abbey of Gethsemani. Used by permission of Doubleday, a division of Random House, Inc. "Poem in the Rain and the Sun," written in 1949 by Thomas Merton, from *In the Dark Before Dawn,* copyright © 1977, 1985 by The Trustees of the Merton Legacy Trust. Reprinted by permission of New Directions Publishing Corp.

Merwin: Excerpt from "Lemuel's Blessing," from *Migration* by W. S. Merwin. Copyright © 1963, 2005 by W. S. Merwin, used by permission of The Wylie Agency LLC.

Millay: "God's World," from her collection *Renascence* (New York: Mitchell Kennerley, 1917): 40-41.

Miller: "To Jesus on Easter," from *Onions and Roses* (Wesleyan University Press, 1968). Copyright © 1968 by Vassar Miller and reprinted by permission of Wesleyan University Press.

Milton: "What in me is dark, illumine," from *Paradise Lost* (Book 1, ll. 22-26).

Mitchell: "The Benediction." Copyright © by the *Christian Century.* "Benediction" by William R. Mitchell is reprinted by permission from the March, 1968, issue of *The Pulpit.*

Montgomery: Composed in Sheffield, England, in 1818, and published in *The Poetical Works of James Montgomery* (London: Longman, Brown, Green, and Longmans, 1856).

Moody: "Here, O Lord," from *The Way to God and How to Find It* (Chicago: Fleming H. Revell, 1884).

More: "The Scribe's Prayer" was More's last private devotion written just before his execution, July, 1535, and preserved in his Prayer Roll, a 1550 copy of which is housed in the Folger Library, Washington, D.C.

Newman: "Stay with me," from "Jesus the Light of the Soul," in *Meditations and Devotions* (London: Longmans, Green and Co., 1893; 1903): 363-365. "Come, O my dear Lord," from "The Kingdom of God," in Newman's *Meditations on Christian Doctrine* (518-521). "Shine forth, O Lord," from *Parochial and Plain Sermons* 4: Sermon 13 (London: Rivingtons, 1875).

Niebuhr: "Many, O Lord," reprinted with permission of the Estate of Reinhold Niebuhr from *Justice and Mercy,* edited by Ursula Niebuhr (New York: Harper and Row, 1974).

Nouwen: From his *A Cry for Mercy: Prayers from the Genesee* (Garden City, NY: Doubleday, 1981). Used by permission of Random House, Inc.

Old: Excerpt from "Blessed you are, Lord God," from *Leading in Prayer: A Workbook for Ministers* (Grand Rapids, MI: William B. Eerdmans, 1995). Reprinted by permission of the publisher; all rights reserved.

Paton: "O Lord, open my eyes," from his collection of prayers, *Instrument of Thy Peace* (New York: Seabury Press, 1968).

Powers: "But Not With Wine," from *The House at Rest,* published by Carmelite Monastery. Copyright © 1984, Carmelite Monastery, Pewaukee, WI. Used with permission.

Quoist: "And so all men," from *Prayers of Life,* trans. Anne Marie de Commaile and Agnes Mitchell Forsyth (Dublin: Gill & Macmillan, 1963). Reprinted by permission of Gill & Macmillan.

Rauschenbusch: From *For God and People: Prayers for Social Awakening* (Boston: Pilgrim Press, 1910).

Rienstra: "A Lament," text original to this collection, with permission.

Rilke: "Du dunkelnde Grund . . . / Dear darkening ground . . . ," "Du siehst, ich will viel . . . / You see, I want a lot . . . ," from RILKE'S BOOK OF HOURS: LOVE POEMS TO GOD by Rainer Maria Rilke, translated by Anita Barrows and Joanna Macy, copyright © 1996 by Anita Barrows and Joanna Macy. Used by permission of Riverhead Books, an imprint of Penguin Group (USA) Inc. "In your long archways" and "I want to record you, observe you," from Rainer Maria Rilke, *The Book of Hours: Prayers to a Lonely God,* Annemarie S. Kidder, trans. (Evanston, IL: Northwestern University Press, 2001): 75, 83. Copyright © 2001 by Annemarie S. Kidder. Reprinted by permission of Northwestern University Press.

Robinson: "Come, Thou Fount," composed in 1757, and appeared in his *A Collection of Hymns* used by the Church of Christ in Angel Alley, Bishop Gate (1759).

Rossetti: "Suppose our duty of the moment," from *Time Flies: A Reading Diary* (London: Society for Promoting Christian Knowledge, 1885). "Lord Jesus Merciful and Patient" and "O most Holy," from *The Face of the Deep: A Devotional Commentary on the Apocalypse* (New York: E. & J. B. Young, 1892): 184; 522. "O Lord Jesus Christ," from *Annus Domini: A Prayer for Each Day of the Year, Founded on a Text of Holy* Scripture (London: James Parker and Co., 1874).

Sarum Primer: The Sarum prayers and devotions developed in thirteenth-century Salisbury. The first version printed in England was in London in 1498; this traditional prayer appears in a 1538 text of that primer.

Schmidt: Text original to this collection.

Selles: "A Writer's Prayer in Autumn," text original to this collection, with permission.

Seremane: "You asked for," from Maureen Edwards, ed., *Living Prayers for Today* (International Bible Reading Association, 1996). Copyright © Joe Seremane. Permission sought.

Service: From "Prelude" and "The Scribe's Prayer," from *Rhymes of a Rolling Stone* (Toronto: William Briggs, 1912): 9-10; 194-195.

Shaw: "He who would be great among you," from *A Widening Light: Poems of the Incarnation,* ed. Luci Shaw (Wheaton, IL: Harold Shaw Publishers, 1984): 78-79.

Smart: "Hymn 3: Epiphany" and "Hymn 15: Taste" were published in *A Translation of the Psalms of David: attempted in the Spirit of Christianity, and adapted to the divine service* (London: Dryden Leach, 1765). "Christ, keep me from the self survey," from *Hymns for the Amusement of Children* (London: T. Carnan, 1771).

Solzhenitsyn: Solzhenitsyn's "Prayer" was written after *One Day in the Life of Ivan Denisovich* (1962) and was widely distributed upon his exile from the Soviet Union. It appeared as "Pominovenie usopih," in *Etioudy i khrokhotnye rasskazy,* copyright © 1996–1998 by Alexandre Solzhenitsyn. This translation is by Aleksandr Solkhenitsyn's son, Ignat Solzhenitsyn. It is published in *The Solzhenitsyn Reader: New and Essential Writings: 1947–2005,* eds. Edward E. Ericson, Jr., and Daniel J. Mahoney (Wilmington, DE: Intercollegiate Studies Institute, 2006): 624-625. By permission of Librairie Arthème Fayard.

Stevenson: From *Prayers Written at Vailima* (New York: Charles Scribner's Sons, 1904): 8.

Stickney: Texts original to this collection.

Taylor: From "Devotions for Ordinary Days," part of his *The Rule and Exercises of Holy Living* (1650). In *The Poetical Works of Edward Taylor,* ed. Thomas Johnson. Copyright © 1939, renewed 1943 by Princeton University Press. Reprinted by permission of Princeton University Press. ("Huswifery," 116; "The Ebb and Flow," 119.)

Tennyson: From the prelude to "In Memoriam A.H.H." (1850): ll. 41-44.

Thomas: "Kneeling," from *The Collected Later Poems, 1988–2000.* Copyright © 2004 by R. S. Thomas. Reprinted by permission of Bloodaxe Books Ltd.

Timmerman: Text original to this collection, with permission.

Topping: Frank Topping, ed., *Daily Prayer* (Oxford: Oxford University Press, 2003). "Most Gracious and Holy Father": 4; "Lord of galaxy and space": 213; "Lord Jesus, write your truth": 62. Reproduced with permission of Curtis Brown Group Ltd, London, on behalf of Frank Topping. Copyright © Frank Topping, 2003.

Tritt: "The Writer's Prayer" Copyright © 1999, Sandy Tritt. All rights reserved. Reprinted with permission.

Vande Kopple: Text original to this collection, with permission.

Vanden Bosch: "A Writer's Prayer after Psalm 144," text original to this collection, with permission.

Vander Lei: Text original to this collection, with permission.

Wangerin: Text original to this collection, with permission.

Watts: "The Heavens Declare Thy Glory," "I'll Praise My Maker," and "Praise Ye the Lord" each from Isaac Watts' *The Psalms of David* (London: J. Clark, 1719).

Wee Worship Book: "Eternal God, whom our words may cradle," excerpted from p. 77 of *A Wee Worship Book* by WGRG, Copyright © 1999, Wild Goose Resource Group, Iona Community, Scotland. GIA Publications, Inc., exclusive North American agent, 7404 S. Mason Ave., Chicago, IL 60638. www.giamusic.com. 800-442-1358. All rights reserved. Used by permission.

Wesley, Charles: "Forth in Thy Name," was originally entitled "Before Work," and was first published in Wesley's *Hymns and Sacred Poems* (Bristol: Felix Farley, 1749).

Wesley, Susanna: "A Prayer for Reverence," recorded as coming from her "original papers" and printed in Rev. John Kirk, *The Mother of the Wesleys: A Biography* (London: John Mason, 1864): 244.

Whittier: "Dear Lord and Father of Mankind," from the poem "The Brewing of Soma," first published in *The Pennsylvania Pilgrim and Other Poems* (Boston: James R. Osgood, 1872): 93-94.

Wiederkehr: "Dear Artist of the Universe," "Make of me a twilight," and "O Word Made Flesh," from *Seven Sacred Pauses* (Notre Dame, IN: Sorin Books, 2008): 177, 179, 62. Excerpted from *Seven Sacred Pauses* by Macrina Wiederkehr. Used with permission of the publisher, Ave Maria Press, Inc., P.O. Box 428, Notre Dame, Indiana 46556, www.avemariapress.com.

Willis: Text original to this collection, with permission.

The Worship Sourcebook, ed. Emily R. Brink and John D. Witvliet (Grand Rapids: Calvin Institute of Christian Worship; Faith Alive Christian Resources; and Baker Books; 2004). "Our Father, forgive us": "Prayers of Confession," #48 (102); "Almighty God, you who shaped": "Advent: Confession and Assurance," #9 (443). Copyright © Faith Alive Christian Resources, taken from *Reformed Worship* 27: 42; 33: 10. Used by permission.

Index

A Reverie

The winds a carol murmur, soft and low,
While silver stars, that gem the arch of night
In answering tones, repeat the choral strain:
Sleep on, O minstrel, calm be thy repose,
Pure as thy spirit, guileless as thy heart;
May golden dreams of past and future years,
Of deeds accomplished, laurels nobly won,
Beguile thy slumber with their magic power,
And bear thee onward to the classic vales,
Where thou in thought hast wandered o'er and o'er,
Hast laved thy brow in sweet Arcadian springs,
And caught the music of Apollo's lyre:
Sleep on, O minstrel, angels guard thy rest,
Till in her chariot drawn by flaming steeds,
Comes the fair goddess of the blushing morn,
And in her beauty smiling bids thee wake.

FANNY CROSBY